THE ENTIRE CITY

A Commentary on Three Texts

IAN DALLAS

Dallas House

First Edition: 2015
Third Edition: Dallas House 2020
All rights reserved

www.iandallas.org

Front Cover: Max Ernst, 'The Entire City', 1935/36. Kunsthaus Zürich, Zurich.

THE ENTIRE CITY

'Oedipe' by Max Ernst from Une Semaine de Bonté, 1934.
Dover Publications, Inc. New York.

Max Ernst, 'The Entire City', 1935/36. Kunsthaus Zürich, Zurich.

'It always happens. "An hundred generations, the leaves of autumn have dropped into the grave." And again we shiver miserably in the confines of a cold winter as christendom and the Roman Empire did hundreds of years ago. Again and again and again we have covered the face of the earth with order and loveliness and a little justice. But only the face of it. Deep down below the subterranean brutes have bided their time to shake down our churches and palaces and let loose the little rats to sport among the ruins.'

[‘Daphne Laureola’: James Bridie: 1949]

'De l’homme il se faisait l’idée que s’en font les gens cultivés et civilisés: qu’il est un être supérieur à l’animal, supérieur a la nature, capable de dominer la nature la pensée et par l’intelligence. Il ne s’était jamais aperçu que l’homme est un fauve.'

[Curzio Malaparte: Le Bal au Kremlin: Denoël 1985]

Contents

INTRODUCTION

This work consists of Commentaries built around three texts:

> Laski: The Historical Introduction to the Vindiciae
> Contra Tyrannos
> Marlowe: The Massacre at Paris
> Dallas: Oedipus and Dionysus

It proposes that what happens in life occurs simultaneously on three levels, the outward, the inward, and the hidden. Be patient. It is not what you have been taught.

Ian Dallas

1

LASKI AND THE VINDICIAE CONTRA TYRANNOS

The first guide on this journey through three political realms is the author of an important analysis of the renowned 'Vindiciae Contra Tyrannos' of Duplessis-Mornay, a document that has resonated over the centuries since its emergence in the epoch of anti-catholic republican thinking which led to the St. Bartholomew's Day Massacre.

Of our three guides, the first only met with me in one casual encounter. The second was for some years a close friend and the third a brief companion in a series of intense dialogues in his Paris art gallery.

As a young writer I found myself on one occasion invited to a weekend at a country house in the Cotswolds. My hosts, with that off-hand English manner that distances but does not fail to affirm social standing, informed me that among their guests was 'someone important in the Labour Party'. He was much more than that, he was the massively influential Professor of Political Science at the London School of Economics. Sitting in the library playing chess with Roger Strauss while the other guests were deep in their bridge games, a forlorn figure drifted in. He spotted my companion, the son of Lord George Strauss, who was a close colleague of Laski in the Labour movement. Having established his discomfort and his questioning as to why he had accepted to be there, he suddenly and dazzlingly turned us into a school of two and taught us why Britain was already doomed to being a servant state of American capital, a fate that would only be delayed but not avoided by Labour's brief intervention in government. It was not a marxist argument. It was about the failure of a state that had abandoned its urge to freedom and justice – he mentioned Milton and Locke, and I knew then at that moment England needed Laski not the fraudulent Isiah Berlin, then the darling of the academics. We never met again. He died shortly after that, dismissed as a Zionist and a Marxist. He was neither at core, he was a Tacitean and an intellectual son of Montesquieu.

Laski opens his Historical Introduction with the annunciatory definition of his work.

> 'All political systems are the natural reflection of their historic environment, and there has been no influential political work that is not, in essence, the autobiography of its time. That does not mean the absence from it of a flavour of universality.'

Laski's ancestors probably took their name from the Primate Archbishop Jan Laski whose blanket authority gave a protective cover to Polish jews under the benign power of King Zygmunt, a ruler who appointed a jew as Treasurer of Lithuania and protected Arian christians who did not believe in the divinity of Jesus. His son, Zygmunt II, on being ordered by a papal envoy to execute heretics, replied: 'Permit me to rule over the goats as well as the sheep.'

(Adam Zamoyski: Poland, a History: Harper) It was from this inherited ethos that Laski, his family at last finding exile and safety in England, began his life's work as a historian and political theorist. If his background established him as a marxist and a zionist it was his historical critique of the state that raised him to the American Republican position, a situation poised in tension between property-owning elite governance and open head-count democracy. The profoundest intellectual influence on the twenty-three year old Laski was to be the then seventy-five year old Supreme Court Judge, Oliver Wendell Holmes. As the ruling, indeed commanding intellectual in England after World War Two, as Professor at the London School of Economics, (Beloff would later define 1920-1950 as the Age of Laski), his core belief lay in Wendell Holmes' position:

> 'The life of law has not been logic: it has been experience. The felt necessities of the time, the prevalent moral and political theories, institutions of public policy, avowed or unconscious, even the prejudices which judges share with their fellow-men, have had a good deal more to do than the syllogism in determining the rules by which men should be governed.'
> ('Common Law': Holmes 1881)

Although a source of academic scandals both in America and Britain, from his early days teaching at Harvard to his days of fame as Professor at the London School of Economics, he never abandoned his conviction that freedom entailed not only the civic ethos but the private world of the individual. By the end of his life two social pillars of his epoch were crumbling, Stalin's dictatorship at the heart of the marxist experiment, and Israel's failure to recognise the Arabs. Now, with that conflict of communism's challenge to capitalism over, and with the dust of old controversies from the 20th century cleared, it becomes possible to view and re-assess Laski as a polemical force challenging the very state itself as a viable machine of human survival.

Writing in 1921 he stated:

'The De Concordantia Catholica of the great Cardinal of Cusa, the Vindiciae of Duplessis Mornay, the De Justa Potestate of Rossaeus – these we must have at our elbow if we are to understand the foundations of the modern state.'

"…we insist by government enactment that personality shall flow along certain preconceived channels. Yet that is in truth to destroy the uniqueness in which the essence of personality consists…. No state can be free which penalises thought. To make political authority commensurate with the bounds of mind is to misread the history of a thousand years."

"The ultimate implication of the monistic state in a society so complex as our own is the transference of freedom from ordinary men to their rulers."

"The political philosopher is concerned with the discovery of motives, the measure of wills, the balance of interests…. He will, in fact, be driven to the perception that, politically, there is no such thing as sovereignty at all…. He will see that, ultimately, the basis of all power is in the consent offered to action by each individual mind: and he may therefore induce the conclusion that liberty is the capacity to resist."

(Foundations of Sovereignty: Laski: 1921)

Amid the ruins and dust of his ancient passions, Lenin's Russia, the Zionist dream, trade unions – without which his thinking would not have been forged – there can now be seen the gleaming jewels of original political wisdom.

VINDICIAE CONTRA TYRANNOS

The Historical Introduction Of Harold Laski

I

All political systems are the natural reflection of their historic environment, and there has been no influential political work that is not, in essence, the autobiography of its time. That does not mean the absence from it of a flavour of universality. Ideas beget a progeny which soon outstrip the narrow concepts of their creator. It means only that the attempt to penetrate the nature of political phenomena has always been coloured by the special experience of the writer. Rousseau is what he is because Geneva retained to the end his ultimate spiritual allegiance; and the federalism of Proudhon bears the marks of one to whom the village of his birth is passionately dear. It is in the competition of the market place that systems receive that correction of the event which gives them their applicability.

This is, in a special degree, true of the Reformation. It was the real starting point of democratic ideas; but, therein, it builded better, or, at least, differently than it knew. In the name of a theory of religious truth, existing ecclesiastical institutions were overthrown; and in the attempt at their reconstruction men were driven to enquire into the nature of obedience. The scale of things underwent a decisive change. European Christianity had previously encountered the notion of reform; it had hardly until the advent of Luther, been compelled to confront the portent of a revolution. The significance of Luther lies in the fact that, all unconsciously, he made the Reformation one of the great turning points in the history of political ideas. From the fall of the Roman empire until his emergence, political thought was always dominated by the notion of a single Christian Commonwealth. Its ultimate sovereignty was the possession of God. Its direction belonged to Pope and Emperor as his viceregents; and the degree of power allotted to each varied with the affiliations of the given writer. The notion of a Europe divided into self-sufficient and independent states was not completely absent; but the universality characteristic of the Church, and the closeness of its connection with political life, prevented that notion from attaining its natural results. The prospect, however, of any genuine imperial suzerainty perished with the failure of Lewis of Bavaria; and when the defeat of the Council of Basle made it clear that any genuine internal purification of Rome was impossible, the way, as Cardinal Cesarini then pointed out, lay open for new political dogmas.

If Luther was not the real author of those dogmas, he was, in a real sense, their efficient cause. Aiming as he did at the reform of the Papacy, conceding, at the outset, the divine character of the Church, it was to a power not less divine in substance that he was compelled to make his appeal. He therefore reasserted the divine character of princely rule; and he deduced therefrom the right of the ruler to control the religion of his subjects. Put summarily, the result of his effort was simply to endow, within the limits of his territory, the Elector of Saxony with papal attributes; and had Lutheranism succeeded without opposition, the result might well have been the extinction of political liberty in Europe. For the sixteenth century is, in any case, a centralising time, and the theory of divine right in princely rule added to despotic notions a religious penumbra at once previously absent from, and curiously alien to, the temper of the religion itself. To Luther, no doubt, the dogma was no more than a weapon forged in the smithy of his special needs; and it had the two obvious merits of attacking the Roman power on the one hand, and beatifying social order upon the other. Nor was it intended to be a radical dogma save against Rome; for Luther, religious doctrine apart, has a place among the great conservatives of history. Yet it was in the discussion of its true meaning that there were evolved the main principles of modern political freedom.

For Luther's protest against the degradation of Rome had synchronised with two other great movements which lent him the aid of their influence. The growth of nationalism in the fifteenth and sixteenth centuries had prepared the ground for the decentralisation of religious power; and the new intellectual atmosphere fostered by the Renaissance made possible the search for, and acceptance of, new religious foundations. But religion was then, and, indeed, until the nineteenth century, too deeply imbedded in the structure of the state for the discussion of religious dogma to be possible without, at the same time, involving enquiry into the validity of political systems. The new religions sought a place within a state that had been previously part of a unified system; and they were prepared to hew their way to acceptance. Once, therefore, research into their rights had been undertaken, the unity of the middle ages was immediately obsolete. Every centre of discontent became also a centre of novelty. The Christian Commonwealth which had been one and indivisible was dissolved into a variety of separate and sovereign states. Men ceased to think in European terms. The interest of Europe as a whole, which had, however vaguely, been preserved above the conflict of nations, was lost before the separate ends of states which viewed their individual well-being as itself the highest objective. The loss by the papacy of any accepted claim to moral leadership was, of course, the main institutional source of change. The idea of the state as the end to be preserved found its justification in part from the renewed contact with Greek political philosophy and in part from the new and pungent sense of immediate fact which is the contribution of the Renaissance to the atmosphere of political discussion. The realism of Aristotle and the pragmatic analysis of Machiavelli combined to defeat the incoherent cosmopolitanism of medieval Christianity. The effort was sharpened by religious warfare; and the new states demanded a new political philosophy for their explanation and safeguard. If they were to be sovereign, they must know the meaning of their sovereignty. Their independence of Rome, on the one hand, and the presence within themselves of dissent, upon the other, made the problem of their internal relationships the main theme of political enquiry.

The sixteenth century is, therefore, nothing so much as one long research into the terms of political obedience. Luther might seek to protect the prince against the anarchy at least in theory implicit in the structure of Protestantism by insisting on the duty of submission to rulers whose power was of God. But that did not bind those to whom his creed was anathema, and, where it brought peace, it was the peace of men who accepted despotism as a relief from war. Yet even then it did not bind those who, coming to full political maturity after the Peace of Augsburg, found themselves outside the narrow boundaries therein laid down for toleration. Had that peace contained some effective measure of protection for the adherents of Calvin, the history of European democracy might have been very different. Dogmas apart, however, temperamental differences between the leaders of Reform made impossible the establishment of a united Protestant front against Rome. The new creed was driven to repeat the belligerent experience of its predecessor.

The result was to throw all political systems once more into the melting pot. Every minority, whether in England or upon the Continent, which struggled against odds for survival, was compelled, by the logic of its situation, to enunciate a theory of the state. It sought to explain its will to live in terms of political right. It challenged the nature of such authority as denied to it a place within the categories of citizenship. Religions which began by protesting that they were entirely innocuous to the existing civil order, continued by insisting that it was the duty of the state to suit its character to the new spiritual dispensation, and they ended by denying the legitimacy of any government which did not admit the merit of toleration. The transformation is well seen in English Protestantism in the movement from Tyndale's Obedience of a Christian Man, with its vigorous defence of passive obedience, to Ponet's insistence, a generation later, upon the right to overthrow a régime which refuses accommodation. The Scottish Reformation was not less prolific of novelty; and it is possible that Buchanan's famous Dialogue was the most influential political essay of the century. As soon, also, as Holland raised the standard of revolt, its thinkers stated a theory of politics in which not merely did the right to religious freedom become a natural part of the philosophy of the state, but the denial of it became the definition of tyranny. Even the magistral effort of Althusius is, at bottom, simply an attempt to generalise from a special situation.

Detail excepted, the method is a similar one throughout Europe. The attempt is always, on the one hand, to limit the power of government, and, on the other, to destroy the papal right of interference by showing the sovereign and, therefore, independent character of the state. This destruction of papal power was not, after 1570, the work of religious reformers alone. There came a time when the civil wars produced by religious dissension had wrought a havoc so extensive that even moderate Catholics were willing to deny that the state must perish for conscience sake. Men were then led to see that state and church can be regarded as species of a larger genus, and that neither is dependent upon the other. That vision, indeed, was partial, and had it not lain at the root of Calvinism in its Scottish form, it is possible that the conversion of Henry IV would have prevented it from bearing its natural fruit. For whether men insist on the definitely separate spheres of church and state, as did Melville and the Presbyterians, or admit that toleration, though a pis aller, is at a certain point inevitable, as did the Politiques, the way lay open for the emergence of a definitely secular state. But that day still lay in a remote future.

The independent character of the state was reached, immediately, in a somewhat different way. It was accomplished by making the use of power a trust, and giving to the people as a corporate whole the right to judge the character of its exercise. The result, inevitably though not deliberately, is a philosophy of the state that has in it the seeds of democratic institutions. For once it is clear that the prince holds his power upon conditions, it becomes necessary to discover the means through which those conditions may be enforced. The merit of popular sovereignty at once becomes apparent; and to an age still permeated by feudal notions, princely power becomes, at least in part, the result of, and dependent upon, a contract with the people. The purpose is not a democratic one; it is the enforcement of some special desire that the contract has always in view. Nor is any loophole left through which the democracy may catch the vision of its power. For, until the reckless days of the League, and then with some vagueness, the corporate people does not mean the mass of individual citizens. It is taken to mean the representative men of the nation, nobles, magistrates, officials, just as, three centuries later, a French Minister could identify the state with the Chamber of Deputies. The notion of equality had not moved from the religious to the political sphere.

This is, of course, unduly to simplify a complex situation; and it omits the influence of such special views as those of Bodin and his school. Above all, it does not sufficiently emphasise what becomes apparent only from the mass of detail, namely, that the favour accorded to popular sovereignty has always a specifically religious penumbra. All successful political generalisations have been intended to serve a particular end; they give to the stereotype of the age a satisfying mythology. As soon as the theory of popular sovereignty had secured for the minority a toleration which, however grudging, was still toleration, the main root of contemporary political disturbance was removed. The partial toleration so won did not, of course, imply that men had learned to accept the secular nature of the state; it implied only, as the Thirty Years' War was, in its origins, to demonstrate, that the cost of religious warfare necessitated a breathing-space in which they learned the political value of indifference. Nor, in general, did they seek to probe further into the meaning of popular sovereignty. It was not until the French Revolution that Europe as a whole grasped the fact that the theory, with all its possibilities, applied not less to political than to religious needs.

In England, indeed, the transition to the secular state had, at least in part, been made much earlier. The Rebellion and the Revolution transferred the results of the discussion upon the place of religion in the state to the political field a century before Rousseau so depicted them that no man might mistake their meaning. But, even in England, until the emergence of Burke and Bentham, it is the consistently religious background of political speculation that is most striking. Locke could not write a treatise on civil government until, in the Letter on Toleration, he had vindicated the self-sufficiency of the state, and its consequent freedom from religious trammels. The implication of the Bangorian controversy was simply, at bottom, that the predominant section of Convocation thought it the duty of the state to persecute in the name of religious truth. Men like Price and Priestley seek so to define the state that they may demonstrate the right of Nonconformists, despite religious difference, to a full citizenship. They and their opponents alike represent the last vestiges of a struggle which goes back to the refusal of Puritan England to accept the system of "Thorough" thrust on it by Laud. But that refusal was not made in the name of toleration, and, in its turn, it takes its form from the long effort to define the nature of a Reformation settlement which refashioned the relationship between state and church. The thought of Tyndale and Ponet, the effort of those, Anglican and Catholic alike, who attempted, under Elizabeth and James I, to discover the nature of political allegiance, these are present, at least by implication, not less in the speeches of Eliot and Pym than in the writings of Hobbes and Filmer. The Reformation, in brief, set the perspective of modern political traditions. It was the chief business of later ages, certainly until the Industrial Revolution, to find institutions best fitted to embody its discoveries.

II

The religious wars of France bring out with especial clarity the real nature of the struggle. Not only did they provoke a crisis in which the very notion of royalty was in danger; they were also a struggle in which political doctrines played a great part in defining and determining the issue. The danger did not come from Calvinism alone. The prospect of a heretic King persuaded the partisans of Rome to the enunciation of dogmas far more extreme than any to which the Huguenots gave adherence. In the shock of conflict, practically every theory of importance in political science until the outbreak of the French Revolution found, in some sort, its expression, with the important and constant exception of egalitarianism. The crisis was, on the whole, unexpected. The firmness of Louis XI, on the one hand, and the easy rule of Louis XII, on the other, seemed to have given the French monarchy a foundation secure beyond all dispute. Yet not only was the succession called into question. The idea of popular election to the throne was mooted. The notion of an inherent, if indirect, right of papal control made itself heard. There were times when the conception of France as a quasi-federation of aristocratic republics did not seem impossible. Once, at least, it seemed within prospect that the estates might seek to transform ancient, if dubious, memories into something akin to the form and substance of an English Parliament. The confusion, of course, did not spring merely from the existence of a Protestant party. It was due, in part, to the economic and social importance of that party's members. In France, as elsewhere, the connection between Protestant doctrine and commercial development is immediate and significant. In part, also, it was caused by the fact that the nobles seized the opportunity of conflict to reassert claims which the previous half-century had seemed to extinguish. The age is hardly less a Fronde than a religious struggle. In part, also, the special circumstances of the struggle, the feebleness of the Kings themselves, and the labyrinthine dishonesties of Catharine de Medici, exasperated men's feelings, and sharpened especially the ambitions of those who, like the Guises, stood within palpable reach of the throne. The hopes of Spain, and the reawakened and reorganised power of Rome undoubtedly contributed to the fashioning of men's thoughts. Yet the existence in France of a powerful body of religious dissent, claiming rights, and with the will to attempt their enforcement in the name of justice, undoubtedly gave to the political ideas of the time a breadth and sharpness of definition they did not have, the work of Buchanan apart, elsewhere. Not indeed that either Catholic or Protestant stood for an unchanging body of coherent doctrine. Each party changed its views with a rapidity that was equalled only by the kaleidoscopic swiftness of events. Protestants who had, under Henry III, embraced the theory of popular sovereignty, had no difficulty, under Henry IV, in proving the virtues of royal absolutism. But ideas have a history more enduring than that of their sponsors. Born of some particular occasion, they live on to become the parent of events far different from what the age of their origin could either have foreseen or desired. The

Huguenot who probably sighed with satisfaction when it became unnecessary to test the adequacy of Hotman's history, the Ligueur who, after the Peace of Vervins, looked back upon the feverish democracy of Boucher and Rose as a bad dream, did not realise that they had released forces more powerful by far than the inert quietude they were so thankful to accept.

To Calvin himself only a very limited degree of political novelty can be traced. Rigidly authoritarian in temper, and without an atom of faith in religious tolerance, it was by indirect means only that he opened the way for the developments that ensued. What he preached was obedience to God, and submission, though at one remove, to the magistrate; and his sense of the importance of authority was clearly shown in his repudiation of Knox to Elizabeth, although he did not clearly recommend any solution when the commands of God and the magistrate were in conflict. The duty of prayer and the acceptance of exile were obvious counsels; but they hardly suited the energy of a vigorous age, and they had the capital defect of involving ruin for those who accepted them. In part, of course, they originate in Calvin's deep, if gloomy, sense of the natural badness of men, and his consequently natural insistence on the virtue of a strong government which should be fortified against the results of their wickedness. Princes, for him, ruled by the will of God and the right of the people was simply the duty of submission. But there was, alongside the power of the prince, the constituted authority of the magistrates, and Calvin came to see that when tyranny is in question, they have the right to invoke resistance. It is clear from the general tenor of his writings that by tyranny Calvin meant a régime which endangered the existence of the new faith. In that event, resistance was simply obedience to the will of God. He seems to have envisaged a situation in which the general rule is submission, and the call to revolt the result of a confidence on the part of those in authority, without co-operation from the mass, that the safety of religious conviction has reached the extreme point of compromise.

So far, indeed, Calvin might well have claimed that his views were simply traditional to his time. Melancthon had previously emphasised the importance of resisting tyranny, and until the massacre of Saint Bartholomew not even the growing severity of the Crown tempted any Huguenot theorist to go seriously beyond that point. What Calvin has to say is little different, for example, from Commines' remark, in the previous age, that God sometimes authorises a revolt against a tyrant. The general background of Calvin's politics is, indeed, hardly incompatible with the theory of the state presented in 1519 by as ardent a royalist as Seyssel. After the death of Louis XII, the despotism depicted by the latter loses its moderation and benevolence, even while the thinkers of the time, and especially the lawyers of the south, continued to insist upon the unlimited nature of royal power. Quod principi placuit legis habet vigorem becomes in fact and theory the motto of the French monarchy; and attractive jeux d'esprit like the Contr' Un of La Boétie would not, before 1572, have provoked any widespread sympathy. A sense of popular right such as the friend of Montaigne depicts is, indeed, as remote from the spirit of the time as the anarchy of Herbert Spencer in an age committed to government interference. The note of all the literature is the unlimited extent of royal power. "The King," said the jurist Vincent de la Loupe in 1551, "can make wars, treaties, and peace when they seem good to him. He can impose taxes, make laws, statutes, and ordinances. He can create such magistrates as he pleases. Whatever he says is accepted as law, and as though it were the oracle of a new Apollo." Nor did the Gallican complexion of French Catholicism do other than emphasise the overwhelming dignity of the King. Du Moulin, for example, did not hesitate, whether as Catholic or Protestant, to admit the royal supremacy over religious matters. When Francis II ascended the French throne, the monarchy seemed securely established in popular acceptance as the pivot of the whole political system. The jurists had given to it the support of legal science. The adherents of either religion had found no discrepancy of importance between dogma and despotism. The change of temper which supervened is as remarkable as it is unexpected.

From the mere existence of religious dissent conflict would not necessarily have developed. Calvinism simply gave rein to a wider controversy which is traceable to diverse causes. There was the memory of Statutes which could be interpreted, as Coke and Prynne interpreted the feudalism of Magna Carta, to narrow the boundaries of royal power. The ancient weakness of the Crown could be contrasted with its recent strength to awaken memories of a time when some degree of popular consultation was the avenue to law. The nobility saw itself deprived of power with deep discontent. Under Louis XI it had been almost annihilated. Under his successors it became a court rather than a magistracy. The people were discontented as a result of foreign war, to them princely ambition meant only the growth of taxes. Nor did the municipalities see the invasion of their prerogatives without the sense that the monarchy had used them for its own exaltation without payment for their aid. The Huguenots, therefore, merely precipitated a controversy of which the possibilities were already latent. Once a party was prepared to make protest against oppression, it was inevitable that every cause of discontent should proclaim its presence, for it is impossible to set bounds to a revolution.

The consequence was that while the Huguenots were striving to prove that the well-being of the state demanded their toleration, and the Catholics to insist that their religion must not be subordinated to purely temporal considerations, each was in fact compelled to envisage the broader political situation in the hypothesis they presented. The massacre of Saint Bartholomew in one generation, and the accession of a Huguenot King in the next, came to give additional point to the dispute. The central dogma involved was not, at first, the sovereignty of the people, but merely the duties of the Crown to its subjects. Once it was discovered that the real problem was not the duties of the Crown, but their enforcement, the theory of popular sovereignty became the real centre of doctrinal discussion; so much so, that even an abstract essay like that of Bodin is, above all, an attempt at its refutation. Not, of course, that it was a new doctrine. Gregory VII had already appealed to it against the encroachments of the Ghibellines. Thomas Aquinas and Marsiglio of Padua had both estimated its validity. In the French wars, it became not merely a dogma, but a dogma supported by battalions, and its analysis was, as a result, something more than academic exercise.

When Francis II ascended the throne, the movement towards popular sovereignty received no direct impetus. Exactly as the early English reformers were almost passionate in their protestations of allegiance, so the Huguenots made a merit of unconditional support to the throne, and they insisted, at a general synod, on the illegitimacy of rebellion. However events were greater than themselves. They had not yet, in any wholesale fashion, been tried by persecution; and their demand for toleration was more the desire to forestall difficulties that were approaching than a protest against the concerted oppression of the government. They were, moreover, gaining ground. Francis Hotman was only the most considerable convert of those won over by the burning of Anne de Bourg. The regency of the Guises united against that disastrous family not merely the nobility, whose pride was affronted by the spectacle of novi homines exercising the sovereignty of the state, but also the Huguenots themselves, who were incensed by the increased persecution for which the Guises made themselves responsible. The result was the conspiracy of Amboise; and thenceforth there was an extending series of outrages until the culmination of all in the massacre of Saint Bartholomew.

The development of political thought does not take the direct line to its obvious goal. None of the earlier rebels admitted that he was attacking the state. He claimed simply to be protecting the King, during his minority, against the advice of evil counsellors. There is, indeed, some evidence that more radical doctrine was slowly gaining ground, although there was no official avowal of a new outlook. Nor did the Catholics think differently. They simply condemned rebellion out of hand. Whether it derived from motives of religion or politics, it was, in their view, always wrong. To this attack the Huguenots replied not, be it noted, by palliating the rebels, but by insisting that the regency of the Guises was unconstitutional. It destroyed, they urged, the foundations of French government. The estates ought to be convoked, and a council provided for the King. They affirmed with emphasis that they were not defending their religion, but simply protecting the Crown. "That only," says one of their pamphleteers, "that only has armed us — it is false to say that our petition to the King masks a religious purpose." Francis Hotman's famous attack on the Cardinal of Lorraine has no other substance than this. Let the people be consulted, as in ancient days, and the throne will be secure against mischance. The sudden death of Francis II followed the official convocation of the estates, but not before Coligny had presented a memorial to the council in which, granted a policy of moderation on the part of the Crown, he offered to pay higher taxes than ever before to prove the measure of Huguenot loyalty to the King.

The reign of Francis II showed no marked change in doctrine, but it demonstrated the existence of two formidable possibilities. It had, in the first place, armed Protestants and Catholics alike. If the motives of rebellion were highly confused, that was less significant than the fact of their presence. It had, in the second place, produced from those whom the Guises had excluded from a share in power, the demand that the Crown be put into Commission during a minority. From that position it would be but a short step to demand some system of perpetual limitation upon monarchical power. The Huguenots, moreover, were building upon the assumption that an unfettered King would necessarily desire toleration. That assumption was bound to prove vain. No King in an era such as this could possibly have remained unfettered, nor was toleration as yet a natural standpoint. What, in brief, had been made clear was that persecution would drive the Huguenots to revolt, and that toleration would involve, at least from those Catholics wedded to the Guises, a grave measure of armed disloyalty. The next years rendered this development inevitable.

Charles IX was only a child; and the regent was Catharine de Medici. She was moved by no purpose save the appetite for power, and she had no policy save that which seemed most likely to maintain her hold upon affairs. For the experiment she embarked upon with Michel de l'Hôpital as chancellor, and toleration as the basis of his government, never had any chance of succeeding. Catharine and her minister were swayed by very different motives. She saw in his policy no more than a means of balancing the power of the Guises by the support of the Huguenots, and when the balance broke down, she had no difficulty in moving to a régime of persecution. L'Hôpital, indeed, took broader views. As he himself said, he was shocked that Frenchmen of opposing religious views should have less in common than foreigners of the same religion; and it was to the rebuilding of the national unity of France that he bent his energies.

The ideas of the author of the Discours de la Réformation de la Justice could not have been applied until a generation of civil war convinced men of their substance. Frenchmen of all parties were still convinced that force was a solution of their problems; they had to pay for their ultimate belief in reasonable compromise by years of social misery. What l'Hôpital preached was moderation in terms of royal despotism. With a theory of monarchy hardly different from that of Seyssel, he sought by administrative skill to conciliate alike Huguenots and Catholics. He realised, as Burke realised two centuries later, that the inevitable outcome of repression is revolution. He saw in Spain what the extreme methods of the Counter-Reformation would produce; and he sought to cut the Gordian knot of metaphysical difference by evading it. He saw that the state could not afford civil war, and his policy was therefore based on the theory that no cause alien to the substance of temporal affairs was sufficient to persuade it to indulgence in such an evil. The theory of royal power for which he stood was too absolute for a nobility which sought a larger share in government, and a third estate which was prepared to defend the retention of urban franchises which acted as a protection for religious freedom, nor were the Huguenots, who counted upon the moderation of his temper, at all wise in the use of their opportunity. For Catharine was the base upon which the pillar of l'Hôpital's conciliation was founded; and the woman who schooled her children in the precepts of Machiavelli was a foundation which needed the most cautious scrutiny.

The true Huguenot policy was silence. But some invited the Queen-Mother to undertake religious reform in time of peace, lest she be driven to attempt it in a time of storm. Others suggested, with more than a hint of threat, that the throne was not hereditary. If these views were exceptional they were important straws in the wind. Nor was this all. The mass of Huguenots were doubtless loyal to the new régime, but some, like Condé, had a conscience whose workings were intimately affiliated to political ambition, and Catharine had learned from her Italian master the proper method with rivals. L'Hôpital could have succeeded only if the results of his policy were not too obvious in the manifest satisfaction of its beneficiaries. The latter were not so wise, and the more extreme Catholics were naturally quick to point out that their own loyalty was affronted by the toleration of heretics. The Chevalier de Villegagnon, for example, was representative of a fairly general temper among his co-religionists when he insisted, in an appeal to Catharine, that the King had sworn to preserve inviolate his religious inheritance, and that to tolerate heresy was to deny his oath. It was hinted abroad that the tolerance of l'Hôpital prepared the way for the conversion of the King, and the Sorbonne accepted the thesis of a young doctor of theology who maintained the view that the Pope could depose a heretic sovereign. Appeal was even made to Philip of Spain to protect the true faith. The temper of all parties was clearly becoming exacerbated. "They begin," wrote the Venetian ambassador to his government, "by showing contempt for the law. Thence they pass to contempt for the magistrate. They end by proving their contempt for the King himself."

L'Hôpital did not improve matters by attempting, in the Colloquy of Passy, to bring together the two religious parties. Théodore Beza, indeed, who represented the Huguenots, spoke with an unwonted conservatism, and explained that his religion made the prince the representative of God on earth. The Cardinal of Lorraine, who spoke for the Catholics, significantly demanded persecution when, with much arrogance, he demanded the defence of the established religion. Nor was it from the Church only that hostility developed. The Parliament of Paris asked why, in the face of law, the heresy of the Huguenots went unpunished, and inquired by what right the King gave them a legal status. The reply made by l'Hôpital that the Parliament should not meddle in affairs beyond its competence only increased the number of his enemies. It was obvious that his ideas of pacification went beyond the convictions of his age and the growing number of conversions to the reformed faith, a number above all significant in the ranks of the nobility, embittered the Catholics against toleration.

L'Hôpital, indeed, had his defenders; but the voice of fanaticism was too loud to be resisted. The Catholics began to publish attacks, to this point without justification, upon Huguenot loyalty. Calvin was shown to favour usurpation; Beza had defended the Conspiracy of Amboise; Calvinism involved — it was an accusation truer than its proponents could then have understood — a federal system destructive of the French monarchy. When the Duc de Guise was assassinated, though the Huguenots in general sought to clear themselves of complicity, some of their leaders, and, most notably, Théodore Beza, spoke in favour of tyrannicide. Catholic indignation grew apace. Exactly as the Huguenots had protested against the persecution of the Guises, so the Catholics protested against the moderation of Catharine and her advisers. They spoke of changing the dynasty, of giving the nobility a larger place in the national councils, of freeing the towns from l'Hôpital's encroachments. The clergy used their sermons to a similar end and it must not be forgotten that the sixteenth-century sermon fulfilled the functions of the modern press. Once the parties had organised, civil war was certain, and with the coming of war there is rarely strength of character enough in any people to permit the expression of moderate views. The position was, moreover, complicated by the fact that the strength of Huguenot organisation, both politically and ecclesiastically, was such as to make them regard the prospects of civil war with some confidence. When Condé took charge of the forces of French Calvinism, he ensured the drift of Catharine towards persecution for two reasons. He was, in the first place, controlled by those who elected him to that office, no happy augury for one who believed in despotism. And Catharine saw in the struggle for religious freedom an avenue through which Condé might seek political power. Her methods, therefore, changed that she might safeguard her position and influence.

The war did not break out without protest and some voices were even raised to demand toleration. It was pointed out by one pamphleteer that God had, over Europe as a whole, protected as well Protestants as Catholics and had thereby manifested his will that both should survive. Castellion, as always urgent in the defence of freedom, insisted that the constraining of conscience never secures more than an empty victory. The curiosity of the time is the insistence of each party on the wickedness of sedition and its desire that the position of the Crown should be kept sacred and inviolate. In fact, the struggle was, in its beginnings, less a direct conflict of religions than a fight between opposing factions of the aristocracy for the possession of the government. The problem of reform happened to be there, and, as the war endured, it became more and more the predominant issue. At the outset, religious difference simply permitted a classification of the contestants, it did not define the objects they had in view.

How true this is becomes clear from Huguenot pamphlets right down to the fatal night of Saint Bartholomew. They are not, they protest, fighting against the King. They merely desire to protect him against the advice of evil Counsellors. They wish to protect the ancient laws of France. They are fearful lest liberty be suppressed. They fight, so they affirm, for the corporate people without distinction of religious belief. In the struggle in which they are engaged, says one writer, they are concerned to protect the integrity of the French throne against the usurpations of the Papacy. The Pope has always been the enemy of the House of Capet, and the counsellors of the King must take thought against the danger he represents. The monarch, it is asserted, is losing the affection of the people, and even if he reigns by divine right, he cannot afford to incur that loss. Another pamphlet draws an analogy between the Huguenots and the famous League of Public Safety. Like the latter, it insists, the Huguenots, as in the great days before the crushing despotism of Louis XI, seek to temper the authority of the Crown by the advice of the nobles, and the corporate will of the provinces and towns. It is, in fact, a species of feudal struggle, and the significance of this enthusiasm for the past is that it emphasises those categories of power in which the Huguenots were most strong. Of their religious demands they say almost nothing. Sometimes there escapes a phrase about the patience they have displayed. Sometimes a note of reality appears as in an attack on the influence of the Sorbonne in promoting civil disturbance. A cry like that of the citizens of La Rochelle that a King hostile to God becomes immediately a mere private person was quite exceptional.

The weakness of this attitude is evident enough. It was the protest of a minority not upon the solid ground of right, but upon the shifty basis of administrative error. It did not frankly avow the substance of its claims, while it sought to conceal the real nature of its efforts in an impossible distinction between the

King and his advisers. For, in theory at least, there was little in this statement of the Huguenot position that an antiquarian-minded Catholic might not have been tempted to accept; and, confronted by the facts as so presented, the Catholic party remained faithful to the Crown. That, indeed, is the substance of its position. Since it was likely to possess the ear of royal authority, its writers devoted themselves to the proof that all rebellion was wrong, and that royal power was absolute by definition. Even a heretic King, said one writer, ought to be obeyed, a significant claim that had, when Henry of Navarre became King, so obvious an application that the Guises procured from its author an explicit repudiation of the idea. Resignation, it is urged, is the only attitude to be adopted in the face of grievance. What the King wills is of God, and to resist him is, as Charles IX said in a proclamation, to forget all fear of him to whom the royal power is due. Nor should the nobility forget how directly its power is dependent upon that of the King. Let the nobles ally themselves with the third estate against the monarchy, said one pamphleteer, and no property will be safe. A single noble with a handful of servants cannot fight a mob of hundreds and the peasants have already begun to attack the estates of the nobility. Let them be once encouraged, as rebellion encourages them, and no one can see the end. Up to the Edict of Longjumeau, the Catholic note is thus moderate, and not unreasonable. If the religious difficulty is largely evaded, that is true also of the Huguenot writers. Astonishment at popular insolence, as with Monluc, insistence that a liberal régime would be disastrous because it would give power to that headless monster an ochlocracy are, after all, no more than the staple arguments of conservatism in the face of popular tumult.

After the Edict of Longjumeau, the atmosphere changes decisively. From the standpoint of Catholic pride, it represented a serious defeat. Catharine saw in it an encroachment by the Huguenots upon her power and there now developed rapidly that desire to be done with reform which culminated in the plans for the massacre. L'Hôpital, still true to the ideal of moderation, was driven from office. His dismissal, indeed, was marked by the publication of a plea for peace which is not the least noble of his writings. To give way to Condé, he urged, is not to capitulate shamefully to rebellion, it is to act as any prince would act who recognises that his subjects are free men. If religious toleration is conceded, the cause of war will disappear. And there cannot, in his view, be political freedom without religious toleration. For liberty cannot be enclosed within boundaries so narrow as to exclude therefrom religion and the conscience it controls. "The liberty of serfdom," he said, "is not liberty at all." L'Hôpital was too late. Catharine had already made her decision. An edict of September, 1568, announced war in the royal name upon the reformed religion. They seek, said the King, to establish an empire within the empire given to him by God. The pamphleteers took on a new tone. It now became a duty to destroy heresy. The contrast between the conciliatory tone adopted by Beza at Passy, and the fact of rebellion was pointed out. The Huguenots did not change. They still protested their humble obedience to the King. Could religious toleration be accorded to them, they were ready to take an oath of loyalty. In reality, their humility was less real than it appeared. In worshipping the King, they had not lost sight of the state of which he was the representative. They equated royalty with freedom, and they meant by freedom not merely the assurance of their safety, but also the preservation of ancient franchises into which the experience of the last generation had driven them to pour a new meaning. What they were in reality seeking was the path to a limited monarchy. Already, there were amongst them men who had blessed tyrannicide. Already, they were discussing whether a prince who did not accept the word of God was a prince at all. Nor was the notion of a contract between monarch and people entirely absent.

They had, in fact, evolved the foundations of a system incompatible with the ambitions of the court. There lay ready to the hand of Catharine de Medici a party to which royal absolutism was a dogma unqualified by any limitation. That persecution was right, they did not doubt, that it should be undertaken, they were ready to prove from the implications, as they deemed them, of heresy. France, they urged, was a Catholic Kingdom, and the King ruled it as an absolute monarch. To say that he did not control the consciences of his subjects was to destroy the roots of his power. Were he to be moderate, the experience of Germany would show him the results of such weakness. Such a policy was bound to commend itself to Catharine as soon as it was clear that the aims of l'Hôpital were incapable of success. To that end Spain and the Papacy were alike endeavouring to persuade her. The Huguenot policy in the Netherlands had failed; and she herself suspected both the ambition of the Bourbons, and the ascendancy established by Coligny over the mind of her son. She made her determination, and there was no difficulty in persuading the weak-willed King to sanction the most extreme plans that Rome could have desired. The die was cast, and on the morrow of Saint Bartholomew, Europe awoke to a new epoch in the history of its political doctrines.

III

The change wrought by the news of the massacre is evident immediately. The court had made the holocaust. Charles IX himself had gloried in its success. It was no longer possible to make any distinction between the King and his advisers. It was the person and position of the crown that was now in question. If Kingship existed for the protection of subjects, what were their rights when the very basis of its meaning was taken away? Saint Bartholomew, as Duplessis-Mornay said, destroyed the mutual faith of prince and subjects, and so uprooted the foundations of the state. It made necessary the abandonment of the fiction that the powers of the King were not a fit subject for discussion. It became essential to survey the rights of citizenship, to discover whether a royal power so obviously capable of abuse, could be permitted to exist without definite and guaranteed limitations. Men did not dream of overthrowing the notion of monarchy, but they had no longer any faith either in the theory of absolutism, on the one hand, or its corollary of passive obedience upon the other. Since Protestantism had been derived from the study of the Old Testament, it became possible to remember the names of Joel and Judith and Jehu. The Catholics might urge that David had refused to be responsible for the death of Saul as the anointed of the Lord. The Huguenots could retort that at least he had, and with divine sanction, taken up arms against his royal master. The New Testament was ransacked for texts which might seem to justify rebellion, and all evidence in favour of submission was explained away. Nor did these researches cease with the Bible. France could not fail to remember that Poland had an elective monarchy. The recent revolutions of Denmark and Scotland were used to point their obvious moral. Harmodius and Brutus became popular deities in the Huguenot Valhalla. The revolt against the tyranny of Tarquin became a model and an example to a horror-struck generation. The issue, for the Huguenots, had become a simple choice between their religious faith and their political loyalty. It was fortunate for European liberty that they did not hesitate in their decision.

Most of the writings which owe their origin to Saint Bartholomew are, on the Protestant side, of two kinds. Some are simple narratives of the day's event. The mere horror of what occurred was rightly regarded as likely to carry conviction of its wickedness to all decent-minded men. Others became, as was natural, a definite enquiry into the nature of government, for it had clearly become essential to restate the Huguenot position. The Court had presented two incompatible defences of its action. On the one hand it had depicted the massacre as the untoward result of a factional conflict within the aristocracy, on the other it had justified, and even boasted of its commission as the necessary consequence of rebellion and a sacrifice offered to the Church. Some Huguenots remained faithful enough to earlier dogma to accept the first explanation. They had then to justify the fact of being in arms and this they did by insisting that while they had no grievance against Kingship itself, they could not bow their necks beneath the yoke of intolerable edicts. Such a position was, of course, an impossible one. It accepted absolutism, on the one hand, while it sought to justify occasional revolution on the other. It was, in fact, the coronation of contingent anarchy and it did nothing to meet the profounder circumstances of the new situation. It had no philosophy save what had already been condemned by the massacre, and its justification of rebellion would have had to be made afresh on each occasion, and then not in terms of general right.

One book then existed of which the substance and temper might have satisfied the most extreme of the Huguenots. The Contr' Un of La Boétie had probably been written twenty-five years before; but the problem it envisaged was exactly the tyranny the Huguenots now confronted. Attractive as was the spirit of La Boétie's essay, avowed and academic republicanism was meat too strong for the digestion of the time. Not that La Boétie was entirely without influence. He was used as cautiously as an Anglican bishop might, in the sixties, have announced an interest in Darwinism. The pseudo-classicism of the French Renaissance never went as far as a disbelief in monarchy. Much more typical was the treatise, now known to have been written by Theodore Beza, on the Rights of Magistrates over their Subjects. The theory of Calvinist politics is here set forth with perfect clarity. To God alone, it urges, does absolute power belong. Magistrates, indeed, have wide authority, and they cannot be held to account by the people. Nevertheless, when they command something that is incompatible with true religion, disobedience becomes a duty, and by disobedience, Beza argues, rebellion may, ultimately, be implied. The value of patience and prayer must not be forgotten; but when the tyranny becomes intolerable, just remedies must be used against it. Not, however, by every member of the state. The ordinary citizen is bound, by the conditions of his citizenship, to submit. The officers of the state, whose business it is to maintain the laws, must secure their authority but they must not depose the prince. There are, however, in each state a body of citizens whose function it is to see that the sovereign does his duty. In France the States-General is a body of such men. They can, if they will, depose the prince. They safeguard the original rights of the people. They may, if they so desire, restore the French monarchy from its present absolutism to a form more consistent with its original and elective foundation. Royalty is, even though divine in nature, essentially dependent upon popular institution. The people has given power to the prince for its own benefit, and, therefore, upon conditions. If the conditions are not fulfilled, it is obvious that the power conferred reverts to the source of its origin. The only thing to be remembered is that the decision of abuse depends upon authorities of a special nature, and cannot be settled by the ordinary citizen.

Though, obviously enough, Beza had French conditions in his mind when he wrote, his book is a purely general treatise. Like most Calvinist pamphlets, it is aristocratic in final texture, and it is wanting in a clear discussion of the exact means whereby the objects Beza had in view could be attained. It is the first pamphlet published during the civil wars of which the main keynote is the idea of popular sovereignty, and Beza may well claim to be the first in that significant procession of those whom Barclay in the De Regno called Monarchomachs. With the Catholic phase of that school we are not, at the moment, concerned, but of the Protestant branch certain general hypotheses may be laid down. In fighting the absolutism of the Reformation State they were concerned to secure religious freedom. None of them valued it as an end in itself. None of them would, had the occasion offered, have conceded freedom to an opponent. Alike in Scotland as with Buchanan, and in France as with Beza and his successors, they were concerned to show the impossibility of an absolute state. They sought to secure certain rights against the possibility of princely encroachment. They had, therefore, to argue, first, that princes are not free to settle as they will the religion of the state, and secondly, that the reason of this limitation lies in the general nature of the state itself. The latter is, for them, practically invariably the result of a contract which, however varied in form, always confers certain rights upon the people. Law is, therefore, never the simple command of an Austinian system, as, for example, that of Bodin, but the attempt to fulfil the purpose of the social contract. If it does not fulfil that purpose, it is not law. Laws, therefore, are the reflection of the law of nature which at once brought into being the social contract and is the purpose and end of political authority.

From the Protestant point of view, the results of this theory are perfectly clear. A law which violates the purpose of the social contract is not a law at all, and may therefore be resisted. Edicts of religious persecution are contrary to that purpose, and the Huguenots, when properly warranted by persons of authority, may take up arms against them. The Monarchomachs had an importance which went far beyond the very limited aim their effort had in view. It was in itself valuable in an age of despotic centralisation so intense as the sixteenth century to have an effective protest against unlimited power. In Scotland, France and Holland the Reformers represented, broadly speaking, a popular movement to which the Crown was hostile. It consequently became the necessary condition of religious success that the aristocracy of the Crown should be secured or some other form of toleration granted. Even in England it is true to say that the condition upon which Parliament was successful against Charles I was the fact that the Puritans were prepared to give battle against the finality of the Elizabethan settlement. The development is, of course, most dear in Holland, where rebellion is not merely successful, but leads to the formation of a republic of which the prosperity was based on toleration. But the Dutch struggle is only the most striking of several, and the whole Monarchomachic movement points the moral that the political liberty of the seventeenth and eighteenth centuries was the outcome of the protest against religious intolerance. Had there not been that protest, the general condition of Europe would have been similar to that of France under Louis XIV — an inert people crushed into uniform subjection by a centralised and unprogressive despotism.

Nor must another aspect of this effort be neglected. The sixteenth century is pre-eminently a century of raison d'état. The poison of Machiavelli was in its blood, and, as the reign of Henry VIII makes evident, a cynical utilitarianism is its predominant temper. Expediency is a basis of rights, it can never become an effective basis of right. It is to the credit of the Monarchomachs that they moved the question to higher ground. They were anxious to make it not merely wise, but also legal, to rebel. In order to do so, they were compelled to show, as in the work of Gentillet, the inadequacy of any basis other than ethical for political institutions. It is permissible to argue that no motive save that of religious conviction would have been strong enough to inspire their effort against the inertia which made men anxious for any peace, whatever its character. They saw clearly that only by meeting the claims of the secular state upon the ground of absolute right could the validity of their plea be accepted. There is no other way in which the rights of associations can be maintained. Once utility is admitted as the sole ground of right, the state can enforce its supremacy as against all other bodies. It is, of course, true that most of the Monarchomachs were aiming at a dominance for their own creed not less complete than that which they denied to the state itself. Undoubtedly the victory of the state was, on the whole, a necessary victory, but its minimisation by religious bodies was the main guarantee against its abuse.

Beza's book is the beginning of a long tradition which expresses itself in many forms. It was at once applied to purely French conditions in a treatise of 1577. The author of Whether it is Lawful for the People and the Nobility to take up Arms is unknown, but it is obvious that he had read Beza's pamphlet to good advantage. Unless, he says, the state of France is remedied, those who love her may well be accused of parricide. They must not confuse the state with the government. The object of the first is the public good, the second may simply seek the welfare of particular persons. With Kingship in particular, it is important to distinguish between the permanent dignity of the office, and the fallible character of some given occupant. If the latter be a tyrant, no one can be so mad as to think resistance to him a crime. Rebellion against tyranny, indeed, is a defence of the real interests of monarchy against those who would destroy it. And the institutions of France have been aptly constructed to this end. The parliaments exercise surveillance over the workings of justice. The chamber of accounts preserves the royal demesne against the danger of excessive alienation. The task of the nobility is to prevent the ruin of the state by enforcing upon the monarch the observance of his coronation oath. Clearly, then, the Huguenots have a right to resist, and when God has made sufficient proof of their endurance, he will not fail to bless their aims.

As a serious defence of the Reformer's position, the pamphlet is at once clear and consistent. Like Beza's essay, it contains within itself the germs of all that was later to be developed into a full and mature theory of the state. Here is set out the notion of a contract between monarch and people, the sense that interference with monarchical power is an ultimate act, for which, however, provision must be made, the conception that power is a trust. The writer is essentially moderate in his outlook. Moved as he obviously was by the spectacle of the massacre, he yet did not seek to erect the circumstances of a very special act of royal perfidy into a philosophy which viewed it as an ordinary event. Like all the Huguenots, rebellion is for him a detestable thing, and authority is always exalted above the reach of the common people. Other writers, intelligibly enough, were less restrained. Some exhausted themselves in vituperation of the government and sought to show, from the analysis of its members' lives, their complete unfitness to rule. The author of La France-Turquie, for example, charges the Crown with seeking to establish a crushing despotism, and in what appears to be the sequel of this pamphlet, he suggests the banishment of Catharine to a convent, the fall of the Chancellor, the exile of the King's counsellors and their replacement by advisers nominated by the provinces, and the dismissal of all foreigners. Until the States-General can be summoned he urges that the towns and provinces of both religions shall form an armed league against tyranny, and refuse to pay taxes. Other writers were deeply anxious for revenge, and demanded any assistance, from within or from without, that might accomplish this end. The author of the Tocsin, for example, was not satisfied to call on Condé and Navarre for help against the tyrant, he summons Elizabeth, William of Orange, and the Swiss, to help in the work of liberation. The author of the Reveille-Matin des Français went even further, and actually appealed to the Guises, the assassins of Coligny, to expel the House of Valois from the throne, and occupy it themselves.

The Reveille-Matin went too far for the vast majority of Huguenots, to embrace the cause of the Guises was only less evil than to see the continuance of the Valois in power. It is more than a mere cri de coeur. Its two dialogues seek to show that Calvinists had been in the history of the previous thirty years devoted to the cause of the Crown, that they had no other object than to assure the well-being of the Kingdom, and the Convocation of the States-General. It speaks with ardent hope of the assassination of the tyrant. It depicts a federal organisation of communes which may by rebellion win their freedom. It insists that the estates may limit the power of the prince. It sees in the maintenance of communal immunities the sole effective guarantee against the crushing effects of monarchical despotism. The book is, to some extent, a compilation. Its account of Saint Bartholomew is taken from a widely-read narrative of Hotman's. Its theories are often an almost textual reproduction of Beza's essay, and its eloquent picture of the disastrous results of tyranny is taken, in great part, from La Boétie. The compiler is uncertain, though it is possibly that Nicholas Barnaud, the physician, whose violence even Beza condemned. It had a wide influence. It was many times reprinted, and it was translated both into Dutch and German. Its appeal to the Guises apart, it differs only in its emphatic tone from the bulk of the writings by the Huguenots produced after the massacre.

They have thus a coherent body of doctrine to enunciate. An insistence upon the validity of tyrannicide. A confidence in the results of a guarantee of local liberties. An appeal to the power of the estates. These are the main part of the common stock of ideas upon which the Protestants drew. With their well-organised municipalities, such as La Rochelle and Montauban, with their closely-knit ecclesiastical structure, with their solid power among the nobility and the rich bourgeoisie, they had every reason to hope that the translation of such ideas into the structure of the French state would be the surest guarantee of their safety. These pamphlets, in fact, were not simply published in the void. They attempted the provision of definite institutional channels for the sources of Protestant strength. What was needed was a convincing proof to their generation that they were seeking not daring innovation but genuine reform. If, like Coke and Selden and Prynne in the next century, they could convince their countrymen that the picture they had in their heads was the original institutional pattern of France before the usurpations of Louis XI, they would immensely increase the power of their appeal. For there is in every generation a large body of men whose zeal for reform is largely dependent upon the degree to which it can be referred to antiquity. If, again, like Locke in the revolution of 1688, they could give to the vague mass of social theory a stability and firmness which made it immediately intelligible to the average citizen, they would become that most deadly of all opponents, a rebellion armed not less with a philosophy than with cannon. So far, the winds of doctrine had blown with equal force on either side. In the next years, and until Henry of Navarre became heir to the throne, the Protestants derived a new strength from their formulation of political doctrine with which the Roman Catholic party was unable to compete.

That strength is not derived entirely from their own resources. Michel de l'Hôpital had seen from the first the vast social loss that would be involved in conflict. Once it was apparent that civil war was not destined to be a mere interlude, the majority of decent-minded Catholics swung round to the support of his ideas. The Politiques, as they are called, are not purely a Catholic party, for Hotman, in his Brutum Fulmen, adopted ideas essentially theirs, and the complicated intrigues of which de la Noue was the centre had as their object the union of Protestants and Catholics on the basis of common effort for a peace of moderation. The importance of the Politiques can hardly be overestimated. It is not merely that their ideas eventually prevailed. Their plea for religious toleration was the root of the settlement worked out in the seventeenth century. Their theory of the relation between church and state was, practically speaking, that through which the state eventually won its freedom from the trammels of medievalism. Their emphasis upon passive obedience and indefeasible hereditary right links them up with the Anglican party of seventeenth-century England. Their literary work is of enduring significance, and though some of it is later in date than the actual struggle in France, all of it has in mind the background of that conflict. The outstanding pamphlets are: the Apologia Catholica of Du Bellay which defends the hereditary claims of Henry of Navarre against the attempt to pervert the succession in favour of the House of Guise, The Satyre Ménipée which is not merely a great satire, but a veritable storehouse of political opinions, The De Regno of Barclay which, while it seeks to overthrow the whole structure of the Monarchomachs, is not the less fatal to the extreme Roman claims, The Quatre Excellent Discours of the Sieur de Fay, the grandson of l'Hôpital, which perhaps best expresses the general feelings of the party, and, above all, the République of Bodin which, though in form a general analysis of political science, is essentially a defence of the position taken up by the Politiques. The speeches of l'Hôpital are an enduring monument to the temper of the movement; while lesser works like the Discours of La Noue and the Vindiciae of Servins are, in a lower rank, illustrative of the diverse aspects possessed by the party. Few things are more symptomatic of the changing temper induced by the Reformation than the rise of the Politiques. Here is a party to whom religion, however individually important, is, socially, a secondary consideration. They made it their business to vindicate the supreme character of the civil power against the claims of any competing allegiance whatever. Their effort was to secure the unity of the state; and they insist that before the demands of such unity all other demands must give way.

Their outlook was purely utilitarian. They defend indefeasible hereditary right and the duty of passive obedience simply on the ultimate ground that the community cannot afford the loss that is implied in the issue to them of a challenge. They favour toleration, not on the ground of right, but because the cost of suppressing diversity of opinion is too heavy to be endured. What above all impresses them is the paramount evil of anarchy. They insist on the removal of religion from the sphere of civil policy on the ground that its retention there breeds an expense that will destroy the state. What they saw clearly was the fact that religious diversity had come to stay and they therefore rejected an ecclesiastical sanction which had ceased to exercise its earlier magic. They were thus driven back to the ideal of a religiously indifferent state as the sole territory on which men could continue to act in concert for the public good. Many, if not most of them, admitted that their ideal was a pis aller. Could persecution have been made to pay, it would have been desirable as a basis for deepening political unity. Once that had been proved impossible, they searched for foundations which should secure order, whatever the cost. This it is which explains their acceptance of divine right, and their passionate defence of the Salic Law. They insist on the necessity of monarchy, and they reject, as with Servins, Hotman and Pithou, the notion that the Pope has the right to control princes. What they established was the self-sufficient and autocratic state of the Grand Monarch. If, in a sense, that was the direct high road to 1789, it is probably an adequate reply that the Reformation had so seriously endangered the foundations of order that their object could hardly have been achieved in another way. It is true, of course, that their exaltation of order at the cost of liberty was itself, as with Barclay, a direct attack upon the Monarchomachs. Here, indeed, their relationship to the latter is not unlike that of Burke to Thomas Paine. The attention of the one was concentrated always on the method by which reform was secured; the attention of the other was directed to the substance of the reform achieved. The Monarchomachs saw only the direct evils of the tyranny beneath which they lived, the Politiques emphasised the cost of overthrowing that tyranny. They were at one with their antagonists in the root of the problem which was the removal of the cause which led the Huguenots to resistance. Once that had been effected, there was little ground of difference between the protagonists of either party. For the Huguenots did not defend resistance to tyranny, and therefore liberty, as such. What they defended was their right to worship God in their own way. Once that had been granted, then substantive grievance was removed; and the enforcement of their general case was left to other causes.

That case was more powerful than they themselves were aware, and even when its particular occasion had been removed, the record remained to serve new purposes. Nor is it doubtful that the impression produced by its mere statement was, at the time, overwhelming. The immense effort made to answer the chief Huguenot writers is evidence enough that they wrote for a generation which responded eagerly to their work. The intellectual power engaged upon the Huguenot side was not the least important lever in its hands, and, in the main, it derived that importance from two works. Much, indeed, of the effort of the Politiques is an attempt to answer them, and it is hardly too much to say that toleration came largely because the Huguenot plea for resistance was the only possible alternative. Of the two books, the earlier was the Franco-Gallia of Hotman. It was the first comprehensive attempt to discover the historical nature of the French monarchy, and therefrom to deduce the rightness of the Huguenot plea for a limitation of royal power. The Vindiciae contra Tyrannos, probably by Duplessis-Mornay, though mainly a brilliant summary of ideas already adumbrated by members of his party, surpassed all other essays of the time in the vigour and lucidity with which it restated them.

Neither book has the appearance, or even substance, of a pamphlet with an immediate purpose. That of Hotman, in particular, with its formidable apparatus of texts, its careful survey of juristic opinion, its analysis of the chroniclers, was hardly less an historical work of the first importance, than a livre de circonstance. It seeks to show that within a time but little beyond the memory of living men, the monarchy of France was elective and controlled by the estates. The men who built the ancient monarchy, the Franks, were in nature, as in name, free. They had sustained their independence against the attack of Rome. If they created a monarchy, they made of their Kings no more than the guardians of their liberties, and to this end, they made the monarchy elective; that was at once a safeguard of good conduct in the monarch himself, and an assurance that he would educate his sons to be worthy of succeeding him. He left to them of right nothing save his personal patrimony. The matter of his succession was decided by the people. Hereditary rule had become a custom. It was directly embodied in no statute, and it derived its value solely from popular acquiescence. In later editions, indeed, Hotman went further and explained how novel was the existing system of absolute monarchy. The title of Majesty, for instance, was accorded to Kings only when they presided over the national assembly. In the edition of 1586, Hotman admits that hereditary succession has become an irrevocable method of royal choice, but since Henry of Navarre had become heir to the French throne in the interval between that date and the first edition, it is unnecessary to suspect any profound explanation of the new emphasis.

Kingship for Hotman, then, has its roots in popular right. It is made by the people, it exists for them. Popular right is not less ample in the organisation of the kingdom. The best form of government is a mixed constitution. That which enables the nobility to be a balance between the competing forces of King and people best secures a régime of liberty. Already, clearly, we have moved far from the facile echoes of Seyssel's theories which had, in the half-century before Bartholomew, satisfied Calvinist writers. This idea of a balance is, in Hotman's view, inherent in the French system through the periodic convocation of the estates. It is to that national assembly that final political control is accorded. It is the guardian of the purpose of the state. Peace and war, the making of laws, nomination to high office, all such matters as these are within its competence. It has regulated the succession. It has prevented the undue alienation of the royal demesne. Without its permission, no King could pardon offenders, or dismiss a high functionary from office. It is, indeed, true that within more recent times the age of popular control has passed, and that of government by lawyers has taken its place. Instead of its national assembly, France is cursed with the Parliament of Paris, a body which is no more than a usurping instrument of the royal will, and, above all, an evil which has come to prominence through the usurping power of Rome, but this is an innovation upon constitutional usage. By right, the national assembly is the guardian of historic French liberties. It was, moreover, supported by the existence of definite and large provincial immunities the protection of which was the purpose of much fundamental law. So, too, with municipal rights. Wherever, in brief, we find the material of popular sovereignty, we find the basis of the French constitution. Its institutions are the channel through which that theory runs, and, where it is obscured, it is because innovation has thwarted its achievement.

The strength of Hotman's book lies not only in the real learning it displays, but also in the very great ability with which it conceals the true object of its polemic. In appearance, it seems to maintain no more than that French absolutism was an historic novelty, and that the true constitution was far more democratic in its operation. But in the process of its argument it is able to buttress every dogma of the Huguenot creed by proving its origin in the facts of French history. Bad Kings may be deposed. The nobility has a special place in the political structure. Women are excluded from a share in government by the Salic law — a palpable hit, not only at Catharine de Medici, but also at contingent Spanish ambitions. The King must be carefully distinguished from the state that the interest of the people may not be confounded with his personal well-being. Local autonomy is the root of political freedom — especially, as in the instance detailed by Hotman, in Languedoc, where Calvinism was especially strong, such provincial freedoms are safeguarded by fundamental law. The whole apparatus of the edifice represented a formidable weapon in the hands of Hotman's party. It made their opponents seem the innovators, while they themselves appeared as the defenders of historic constitutionalism. Nor can the Catholic answers to the book be said to have disturbed its central positions. Papire Masson, the royalist historian, could find no more than invective as a retort to its argument. Matharel, one of the writers whose fortune had been made by abject subservience to Catharine de

Medici, attempted a refutation point by point; but he lacked the knowledge necessary to his task, and was driven to rely upon abuse of plaintiff's attorney. Zampini did, indeed, make Hotman's intransigent position upon the Salic law appear an overemphasis; but he was overwhelmed in the ridicule of Hotman's reply. The best answer came from a Paris lawyer, Turrellus; but he could do little more than demonstrate that Hotman had, in a variety of places, refined unduly. It is not, on the whole, untrue to say that the Franco-Gallia remained the classic exposition of early French institutions until, in the second quarter of the nineteenth century, Augustin Thierry began his scientific study. Attacks in which Matharel and others sought to show the evil effects of popular rule were, of course, beside the point; for Hotman had chosen to occupy different ground.

It was to the question of the validity of popular right that the Vindiciae contra Tyrannos was addressed. Immediately, it appears probable that the work of Hotman had more effect. In the long run, the greater interest of Mornay's pamphlet is as certain as its greater influence. So, similarly, the scholastic involutions of Occam's Dialogus had interested his generation far more than the direct brevity of the Defensor Pacis. Just as the very width of Marsiglio's generalisations gave them a more permanent influence than the labyrinthine theses of Occam, so because Mornay summarised the result of the conflict with telling simplicity, it was to his arguments that a later age turned.

The Vindiciae deals directly with the four great questions of the time. Are subjects bound to obey princes if they command that which is contrary to the law of God? Is it lawful to resist a prince who infringes the law of God, and ruins the Church, and, if so, who ought to resist him, by what means, and how far should resistance extend? Is it lawful to resist a prince who ruins the state, and, if so, to whom should the organisation of resistance, its means and limits, be confided? Are neighbouring princes bound by law to help the subjects of princes who afflict them either for the cause of religion or in the practice of tyranny? To the first question, the Vindiciae responds in the negative. It is clear from the authority of Scripture and the example of the martyrs that the commands of God merit obedience before any orders from an earthly prince. Nor is this situation altered by the fact that princes claim to rule by divine right. The earth is the possession of the Lord, and Kings reign only by his will. One must then obey them only to the degree that they obey the commands of their master. The King is a vassal like any other vassal. He is, therefore, bound by a contract. Should he break its terms, diffidatio ensues, as it would in any other case. The establishment of Kingship, in fact, clearly involves a double contract. There is a contract between God, on the one hand, and the King upon the other. There is a contract also between the King and the people. Clearly again, therefore, whatever binds the King binds the people also. Should the King fail in his duty, the people must not forget its obligations. To obey its earthly master in preference to obedience from God is to invoke the punishment of heaven, for when men fail to obey the laws of God they are expelling him from his Kingdom. The King is instituted only to secure the better observance of those laws, and, when he fails, his sin ought not to involve popular acquiescence. That, indeed, is the true rebellion. It is as though men obeyed an officer rather than the express ordinance of the King himself. When subjects refuse to give their conscience into evil keeping, they obey the true source of right. For there are, as Cicero said, degrees of duty, of which the highest belongs to God, and the second only to one's country; just as in the civil law, treason, though it be a heinous crime, is inferior in wickedness to wrongdoing. Nor do the Apostles write otherwise.

It is one thing to refuse obedience to a command which infringes the will of God. Whether one ought to organise resistance to a prince who seeks to infringe it and attack the Church seems, at first sight, a more difficult and complex question.

Yet in appearance only. For the people have, jointly with the prince, made a contract with God. They are like a debtor who has a joint obligation to pay a certain sum. Should the other party fail, the entire debt falls upon the remaining signatory. Just as the Jewish people was bound to God, and was warned by the prophets of its duty whenever Kings strayed from the divine path, so also is the Christian people bound. The contract has always involved a popular obligation. Too much danger was risked in committing the custody of the Church to a single person. A people affected to true religion will, therefore, feel itself driven both to reprove, and, if need be, to repress a prince who would destroy it, for they will know that in neglecting to perform this duty, they make themselves guilty of the same crime, and will merit, as they will receive, the same punishment. But to say that a whole people must resist does not mean that so many headed a monster as the multitude has the duty of revolt. By the people is meant their chosen magistrates who represent, and mirror within themselves, the will of the nation. It is their business to restrain the encroachments of the prince and, in the last instance, to exercise a final control. Every well-ordered kingdom has an authority of this kind, commissioned to speak in its name. It is composed of the natural heads of the state, and, once they decide to act, whatever they will is good, granted only a worthy object as the purpose of their decision. Nor need they hesitate to act, even when, as in the case of the Maccabees, the whole nation is against them. The contract that binds the whole people binds its parts also, just as in Germany each prince and free city is separately bound in fealty to the empire. When a city or a prince refuses obedience in such a case, it absolves itself from membership of what is, in fact, simply an assembly of brigands rather than of Christian men. For where there is no justice, there is no commonwealth, since justice is the virtue which gives to each his own, yet here, by definition, the prince is depriving God of his heritage. So the Sorbonne and the Parliament of Paris sanctioned the decision of Philip the Fair to cease connection with the papacy of Boniface VIII when the latter sought unduly to extend his prerogative. So, also, the Assembly of the French Church refused to obey the schismatic pope, Benedict XIII. It is high treason against the divine authority for men in positions of trust to act otherwise.

What engages the community as a whole through the persons of its magistrates does not similarly bind the private citizen. Unless he is specifically called by authority to revolt, his allotted task is passive resistance only. For what is required of the whole does not bind each unit of the whole in its private aspect; what, on the contrary, the Scriptures enjoin upon the private citizen is that he shall put his sword into his scabbard. He must do as the faithful did when Jeroboam abolished the service of the true God, and suffer voluntary exile. It is only when the official call comes that he is permitted to resist by force. If each man were to follow his own conscience, there would result not only confusion, but the fatal deception which comes from man's willingness to mistake his private desire for the will of heaven. When the call does come, the citizen need not fear that the use of arms is unlawful. The number of good princes who have by force of arms defended the service of God against the pagan is infinite. The Apostle himself has told us that the magistrate does not bear the sword in vain. To what better use could he devote it than to the service of the true faith? Even more, it is his duty to take to himself every weapon that may fortify the vine of Christ against the wild boar of the forest that seeks to uproot and devour it. It is his business to be armed for virtue.

The case, therefore, is clear, where the interests of God are directly in question. The magistrates may authorise resistance by force to the prince who seeks injury against the true church. Are the same principles applicable when the interests concerned are of a purely temporal character? Here we meet the central problem of politics — the general nature of the obedience due to princes. The latter are instituted by God, but they owe their power to the people, and they exist only that they may bear upon their shoulders the main burdens of the commonwealth. The choice of a King is a matter everywhere of popular election. Even though hereditary succession has long been the general custom, the ceremony of the coronation, in particular its oath, remains to show that Kingship rests upon popular choice. The King, therefore, is the delegate of the people for specific functions. The people is greater than the King, and he can have no power save that which it confers upon him in the purpose of his institution. The consent of the people is like the base of the Rhodian Colossus; when it is withdrawn the statue crashes into the dust, and, as with the prince, so with the officers of the Kingdom. They are the servants, not of the King, but of the people. Their nomination derives from the authority of the state, and they are charged to protect, not the personal interest of the prince, but the public interest of all. Once, indeed, they consulted the whole people; now they are bound only to obey its representatives. It is true that officials have, in recent times, seemed to possess only the shadow of their former power, but the development of princely absolutism is not effective against popular right. Time cannot confer a prescription against the people.

Popular sovereignty is therefore the basis of royal power. How far does that power extend? Since an institution is good only to the degree to which it fulfils the purpose of its existence, it is from the scrutiny of the latter that the limits of royal authority may be ascertained, but in so speaking we make absolutism impossible; for it is with limits that we seek the foundations of power. It is with limits because men are by nature apt to the love of liberty, and it is sufficiently obvious that Kingship is maintained because, and only because, they believe in the benefit it confers. What they sought in its establishment was safety from external attack, on the one hand, and freedom, on the other, from the internal conflict which results from the institution of property. The business of the King is thus to make war, if need be, and to render justice. He must preside over the courts, and see to it that the law is supreme there. The maintenance of the law is the very soul of his function. He does not create it. He merely gives it support. Law is the embodiment of reason, and so free from the human passions, to which he is subject. To the law, within which, let it be noted, are comprised the liberties of towns and provinces, every King must give obedience. Should he abrogate the law, it can only be on condition that the people, or their natural leaders, are consulted and acquiesce. He cannot punish, save in accord-ance with law. He cannot otherwise pardon. He can dispose of the private property of his subjects only as the law permits. Nor, similarly, can he alienate the royal demesne, he has its usufruct, but he is not its owner. He has its usufruct to maintain the state of his office, just as he has taxes for war and other public needs. He is, in short, merely the administrator of the royal demesne. He has the same power over it as a bishop over the property of his diocese. He is the trustee of a temporary possession, a trus-tee who may always be held accountable for an abuse of trust. Accountability, in fact, is inherent in the nature of his function, for a people which sought safety would not submit itself, in any absolute fashion, to the caprice of a man endowed with the same passions as ordinary humanity. To leave him free to make laws or confiscate private property at will would make his relations to his subjects that of a conqueror to the enemies he has laid low.

Every Kingdom, indeed, bears witness to the truth of this conception, for in every Kingdom there is some sort of covenant between prince and people. The ancient Kings of Burgundy swore to protect all men in their rights according to law and justice. The ceremony of coronation in Aragon not only implied a higher majesty in the commonwealth than in the crown, but also implied, should the coronation oath be broken, the exemption of the subject from allegiance. Two sorts of tyrants must be distinguished. There is the usurper whose power has no basis in right. He invades the country of his neighbours in the sheer lust for dominion, or he may, by corruption and deceit, worm his way to the throne. Sometimes the usurper has been, like Julius Cæsar, a popular general. Sometimes it has been a woman who has intruded her presence into a government from which she is excluded by law. Such a tyrant may be killed by the simple citizen without the authority of the magistrate, for in combating one who stands by definition outside all categories of law, it is life and liberty in their elementary terms that he is concerned to defend. The second form of tyrant is the prince who, though reigning by legal title, neglects the contract to which he is bound by the terms of his inception. His proper treatment is a more difficult matter than in the first case. We must make allowances for the fact that, being a man, he is likely to err. We must therefore first seek, by reasonable means, to lead him to the path of right. The wisdom of a senate may well enable a naturally weak prince to govern well, but when, of set purpose, the prince is determined to pervert justice and equity, force must be used against him, and it is the officers and nobles of the Kingdom whose business it then is to exact a remedy. That is the reason for their existence, and if they fail, they share in his crimes. In destroying his tyranny, they act on behalf of the state. They protect the humble who, in this instance, have no function save that of resignation, against the wrongs he would commit. They secure the observance of the contract he has made with the state. As a general council may be summoned to protect the Church from the consequence of papal crime, so must the officers of the Kingdom ever remember that if the King has the first place in the realm, theirs is the second. And they are a second who may become the first, for they are the reserve power of the Commonwealth.

There remains the final question of the prince who sees the citizens of another country oppressed either for religious or political causes. What duty is laid upon him? In matters of religion, there can be no doubt that he is morally bound to intervene, for there is only one true Church, of which Jesus Christ is the head. Should its members be injured, the whole Church participates in the harm and sorrow which result, and since the care of the Church is recommended to the charge of Christian princes in general, they must not merely amplify and extend its boundaries where they can, but also, and in all places, preserve it against attack. So Josias expelled idolatry from the Kingdom of Israel, even though he was then in subjection to Assyria. So Constantine executed Licinius for his persecution of the Christians. So Moses bound certain tribes beyond the Jordan to aid the Israelites against their enemies, and pronounced an anathema against them if they should fail. Nor is the case less clear in civil matters. Princes are, after all, men, and the duties of humanity are fit and convenient for them. A private citizen is called upon to help a neighbour who is beset by evil men, how much more, then, is it incumbent upon a prince to act in similar fashion? If he finds a commonwealth grovelling upon the floor, let him raise it to its former eminence. It may well be that his private interest persuades him to stand aside, but nothing so much becomes a man, even more a prince, so to dispose his actions that his private interests give place to public need. No prince would hesitate to give assistance to a brother monarch in distress. How much the more readily, then, should he aid a whole people, when the affliction of many is so clearly the cause of a greater pity. Charity challenges him to the relief of the oppressed, as justice requires that a tyrant be compelled to reason.

IV

In the sixteenth century there are two main forms of political doctrine, of which the République of Bodin and the Vindiciae of Duplessis-Mornay are perhaps the best examples. In the one, the main effort is to find a juristic basis for raison d'etat. The root of political wisdom is therefore an unlimited sovereignty which makes a command into law by the mere supremacy of the person from whom it emanates. The true example of law is therefore that positive enactment which is embodied in legislation. The essential thing is that the command shall be supreme, irresponsible, and unhindered by the scrutiny of conditions. It is true that reference is made by Bodin to laws of nature, of God, and of nations by which the ruler is bound. As Hobbes was later to point out, since the prince is the only person who can, in this context, enforce obedience to them, the essence of the theory is the unlimited nature of the sovereign power. The real result is to separate ethics from politics, and thus to complete by theoretical means the division which Machiavelli had effected on practical grounds. The state becomes supreme upon its own territory, and the expression of its will is law. And the attempt to introduce moral limitations upon the exercise of that will becomes clearly impossible. All associations become contingent upon its pleasure, and right is to be defined as that which the sovereign permits. Jus est quod jussum est becomes the definition of the state. The characteristic of an organised political community is the existence within it of an authority which is not only habitually obeyed, but is itself beyond the reach of authority. Right becomes, so to speak, pluralised into rights. It is no longer the reflection of a universal good, but a series of privileges to be discovered in the statute-book. The state must be obeyed upon the simple ground that it is a state.

It is easy to understand the attractiveness of this theory to the age which enunciated it. The medieval prince was only a greater noble whose power was limited on every side by the special immunities of church and feudalism. The age of the Renaissance brought changes so swift and catastrophic that men welcomed any authority which guarded, or seemed to guard, the possibility of order against the flood tide of anarchy. Its attractiveness was intensified when, as with Henry VIII, the sovereignty of the state could find its incarnation in a prince whose power was immediate and obvious. Here was something, as Barclay always insisted, which, however evil when it entails tyranny, is nevertheless superior to the evils which insurrection brings in its train. The theory of Bodin may not have meant the realisation of abstract right, any more than the existence of the courts implies the realisation of justice, but it implied the existence of certainty. Men had learned from the previous age rather to be content with an imperfect good than to seek the texture of that perfect commonwealth upon the substance of which so few of them were agreed.

The doctrine of the Vindiciae starts from the antithetic standpoint. It is with the establishment of abstract right that it is throughout concerned. By abstract right it means, at bottom, the will of God, and everything is illegitimate which transgresses its substance. Where Bodin, therefore, is concerned with the irresponsibility of supreme power, Duplessis-Mornay is concerned with its limitations. Where Bodin seeks to show that rights are the creatures of the sovereign will, rights, in the other view, are the reflection of right and therein is to be found the only true source of sovereign power. To Bodin, therefore, the thing of main importance is simply whether the enacting authority is, in the given instance, competent to act in the way it has acted with the inference that if the authority is the sovereign, it is competent without further scrutiny. To Duplessis-Mornay, on the other hand, the crucial point is not the willer, but the substance of the thing willed, and if that substance, when it contradicts divine law, is maintained, it must be resisted at all costs. In the strictly political sense, therefore, there is really in the Vindiciae no such thing as sovereignty at all. We are given right and power, and rebellion is interposed to mark the extreme limit of divergence between them. Power does not carry with it any political connotation. It is there because God and the people so will it. The people which created it is morally obliged to scrutinise its operation, and they must overthrow it in the event of abuse.

The hold of the Vindiciae upon not merely its own, but the later generations which absorbed its substance, was, of course, the fact that it gave an obvious means of resisting what any given group of men might choose to regard as oppression. Revolution was, in that age, the only weapon to oppose to religious intolerance. To men who were being taught by lawyers and learned men that the fiat of the state was enough, it seemed to place rebellion upon the ground of right. To the Politiques' cry of convenience it replied with a plea of moral duty, and when that plea was surrounded by a religious atmosphere passionately felt, it was sufficient to convince. Nor must it be forgotten that, in the strict realm of theory, Bodin was the innovator and Duplessis-Mornay the guardian of traditional doctrine. For his views of the ground of obedience sprang full-grown from the noble medieval concept of the world as governed by natural law. What he was doing for his readers was to refer the actions of the state to the test of an eternal reason which sprang from God and was instinct with his will. All other laws than this were therefore secondary because they sprang from fallible men. When Bodin and, later, Hobbes were striving to make of law simply the command of a sovereign power, they were running counter, as their opponents at once recognised, to the whole burden of medieval notions. Duplessis-Mornay was insisting that important as is civil society, and not a little of his influence comes from his emphasis upon its importance, there are interests higher than those of the state for which no sacrifice is too much. Government, for him, is thus ultimately a theocracy. It follows that when the human administrator is in conflict with the divine ruler, the citizen can really have no hesitation as to where his obedience must lie.

It is, of course, easy to criticise the structure upon which the Vindiciae depends. It does not explain the origins of the state. Buchanan and Mariana apart, indeed, it is a capital fault in all the Monarchomachs that they assume the existence of the state and then explain its primary assumptions in terms for which they offer no historic warrant. For their dependence upon the theory of a social contract lays them open to all the objections raised since the time of Hume to that disastrous hypothesis. Nor is that all. The whole view of the Vindiciae is built upon the assumption that it is the duty of the magistrate to represent the popular idea of right. It has nowhere any rigorous examination of the representative principle. The Vindiciae, indeed, makes the people sovereign, but in such a fashion as to make its supremacy meaningless save where it is governed by a tyrant who has usurped his power. It is represented by magistrates. It is admitted that as a matter of contemporary fact, the magistrate has his commission from the very ruler he is supposed to control. No one, in fact, can read the Vindiciae without being impressed by the meagreness of its concessions to the people. The latter is an originating but not an active agency. Duplessis-Mornay shares to the full the characteristic Huguenot contempt for the people. He is like a whig aristocrat of the eighteenth century who welcomes popular support but does not concede to it a share in government. He identifies the people with the state. The only purpose of the people is to serve as an agency of origin which justifies the resistance of the aristocracy to what they consider an abuse of power. He is not, like Althusius, writing an ample theory of the state. Clearly, at the back of his mind there is the single problem of religious oppression. He sees that the principles he lays down apply to civil not less than to ecclesiastical problems, but he is not anxious unduly to enlarge their boundaries. Like all the Huguenots, he uses the Bible as the obvious source of social truths. It is not without significance that it is the discussion of civil problems that is least grounded in biblical authority. Probably, indeed, the secular aspect of oppression was for him essentially the derivative of the religious. It then becomes clear why Duplessis-Mornay could, on the cessation of the latter, revert like Hotman to a belief in the divine right of Kings. Yet these limitations and inconsistencies impair neither the impressiveness nor the influence of his book. Eighty years after his death a German publicist could declare that he and Althusius more easily seduced men to bad principles than any other writers.

The more immediate heirs to his theories were not his friends, but his opponents, even if democratic government was in a real sense his residuary legatee. For with the death of the Duke of

Anjou in 1584, Henry of Navarre became the heir apparent to the French throne, and the certainty that a Huguenot King offered a greater opportunity to the reformed religion than explorations into the realm of the abstract, turned its adherents into thorough-going supporters of hereditary right and the Salic Law. The defence of radicalism then passed into the hands of the League and the Jesuits. What the former was striving to prove was the theory that no heretic could ever be lawfully King of France, and it relied for proof upon the doctrines of the Vindiciae. Just as the advocates of papal dominion had always admitted that a papal heretic can always be deposed, so do the advocates of the League urge that an heretical King is by definition a tyrant and therefore by definition unacceptable. The literature in defence of this position is more remarkable for its quantity than its quality. The pamphlets of Louis d'Orléans, indeed, have some merit. The sermons of Boucher explore with some eloquence the half-known hinterland of invective. The Dialogue du Manant et Maheustre shows that behind the unworthy ambitions of the Guises and the preachers there was, struggling for survival, a notion of theocracy that is not devoid of nobility. Perhaps the most characteristic product of the Catholic Monarchomachs is the True Power of a Christian State of Rossaeus. It is usually attributed to that Rose, the fanatic bishop of Senlis, who is so severely handled in the Satyre Ménippée; but, as Labitte has shown, the grounds for any attribution are extremely slender, and it is better, perhaps also kinder, to leave its authorship in the pale realm of anonymity.

How dependent Rossaeus was upon the substance of the Vindiciae is apparent from the merest summary of his teaching. He insists upon the naturalness of civil government, which is inherent in the nature of men. No special form of government was established; the constitution of each society has always been dependent upon the pleasure of the sovereign people. Where it has established Kingship, it has always been upon the contractual basis of retaining ultimate power in its own hands and defining that conceded to the prince by the purpose he is to serve. The people can always modify the government which depends upon its will, and it can even, if it pleases, abolish monarchy altogether. The prince has no rights save those he possesses to fulfil the purpose of his institution, and if he plays the tyrant he must be deposed. Consultation of the people is fundamental, for the people has not parted with its original freedom. What it has established, it builds only for the attainment of good. Once the King fails to secure it, his commission is clearly revoked. But good cannot be secured without religion. Rossaeus does not mean by religion any form of Protestantism, either form is worse than paganism. Any government, therefore, which fails to establish the Roman Catholic religion is, ipso facto, illegitimate. A heretic King may, therefore, be deposed, either by his own subjects, or by a foreign prince, for he is by definition a tyrant since his heresy is incompatible with the maintenance of virtue.

Nor must the immediate background of Rossaeus be neglected. The Vindiciae had pointed its moral for contemporary events by the implications it contained. Rossaeus has no hesitation in saying openly what is in his mind. Turks and Saracens have more rights than the Huguenots, who are French only in the sense that a dog is called French. Henry IV can never be a Christian King. He is the worst of traitors. As an excommunicate he can take no oath, and the toleration he would establish is the first step on the road that would lead to the recognition of Islam. He is a heretic, and all history and scripture testify that it is legitimate to take up arms against him. He is a tyrant, and the way to treat him was shown in the noble act of Jacques Clement when he murdered Henry III in defence of the Church against the wicked plots of the Politiques. The duty of all Frenchmen is to obey the call of the League. It is supported by Spain. It has as members the Cardinal of Bourbon, who is the rightful King, and the House of Lorraine. If Henry IV is maintained in power, all property will be unsafe. The nobility will be merged in the populace, and lose all influence and position, for Calvinism is incompatible with Kingship and aristocracy. Its secret plan, indeed, is to make the government of France like to that of Switzerland. It is already, in its ecclesiastical organisation, an imperium in imperio. Should it be tolerated longer, the true France will perish.

Clearly enough, the Catholic and Protestant Monarchomachs approach the same problem from different sides. Each party was hostile to the absolute state in the one case because it presaged, in the other because it denied, religious toleration. Each sought relief from its trammels in considerations of right, and each sought to defend the maintenance of right by means of a social contract derived from the sovereignty of the people. Each was at bottom entirely indifferent to freedom. The Catholics aimed quite definitely at persecution. The real effort of the Huguenots was, as Rossaeus himself pointed out, a desire to found such a Presbyterian tyranny as Calvin established at Geneva or Knox in Scotland. Both, that is to say, failed to grasp, as the Politiques had definitely grasped, the notion of the state as a self-sufficient society of which the ethical roots were to be discovered within and not without itself. With both, of course, the contingent implications are far wider than the conscious purpose. Each of them was really puzzled by the single problem of allegiance. They sought to deny the duty of obedience when it involved results unfavourable to a given religion. To a philosophic theory of the state neither could make pretence. Their weapons were too entirely at the service of their desires for it to be as yet possible for them to attain that degree of obstruction at which a philosophic view alone becomes possible. Yet each was making generalisations which, in other hands, would move towards that end. The Monarchomachs are summed up in Salamonius and Althusius on the one side, and the Society of Jesus on the other. The Monarchomachs may have failed to realise all the profits of their thought, but at least they provided the materials for the next generation. The real inheritors of their work are, in fact, the Jesuits and the English thinkers of the seventeenth century, for the thought of the time is hardly national, but European, and the two streams of doctrine blended into a common tradition. The Jesuits, of course, had a different aim in view. As the chief agents of the Counter-Reformation, and, in particular, the Spanish theory of it, they were no more concerned with the roots of freedom than their predecessors. But they were confronted with a Europe that was religiously heterogeneous. They used the Presbyterian hint of two societies, religious and secular, with concurrent jurisdictions over the same persons as the clue to their purpose. From this they are able to deduce the view of states as independent, equal, and sovereign which, in the hands of Grotius, made possible the development of international law. The independence, indeed, is never real. There is always, as in the famous book of Bellarmine, the indirect power of the pope outside to destroy its logical result.

They did, the needs of religion apart, emphasise more completely than any other group of thinkers the fact that civil society is a natural product of men's dispositions, that power is organised to serve its purposes, and that power is, as a consequence, always popular in origin that the purpose of its institution may be preserved. The Jesuits did not get so far as Althusius in their sense of the corporateness of communities, with the personality to which that corporateness gives rise, but they did see that political power is the result of social facts and that it remains the eternal possession of the people. The prince for them is always the mere administrator of those institutions which fulfil the end of civil right, and absolutism is ruled out as a priori impossible. They use the notion of a social contract, but it has not, with them, as it has in the writings of the Monarchomachs, anything like a primary importance. Their governing concept is natural law. Power is always regarded as limited so that eternal reason, which popular sovereignty is held ultimately to embody, may correct the deficiencies of its exercise.

It is clear that this is in the direct tradition of the Vindiciae. It retains, of course, an ultimate religious perspective, and the state is made as subservient to the ends of the Roman Church by the Jesuits as it was made to minister to Huguenot demands by Beza and his disciples. Its translation into a predominantly secular theory was mainly the result of the seventeenth-century struggle between King and Parliament in England. Of that evolution John Locke supplied a magistral summary, and he did little, the theory of toleration apart, but adapt the teachings of the Vindiciae to an English atmosphere. With him, as with his predecessors, there is the same suppression of the idea of sovereignty, the same confinement of the law-making power within a previously defined area of capacity. Like them, too, Locke thinks of the state as a human, even an artificial contrivance. He cannot believe that man surrendered his rights to it save in terms of a previously guaranteed return. Power for him is just as much a trust revocable on abuse, as it is with the thinkers of the sixteenth century. He has the same dread of absolutism, the same refusal to make the final nature of social life depend upon some naturally inherent and coordinating power in the state. The atomism of the Vindiciae is, in fact, as notable in Locke as in the earlier exponents of the contract theory, and not unnaturally, for with him also the main purpose of the polemic is to set bounds to the power of government. The absolutism of the sixteenth century was attacked because it was found to be incompatible with freedom of religious belief, the prerogative of the seventeenth found opponents in those who sought a larger degree of national self-determination. Both ages found the defence of their position in the concept of a state built upon the rights separately surrendered by individuals. Those rights were a matter of contractual organisation, and for the state to step outside the boundaries they defined was to deny the character of its origin.

Practically, this is to say, the theory of the state upon which the Vindiciae rests determined the character of political speculation from the end of the sixteenth century until the advent of Rousseau. So long as the aim of political philosophy was to outline the area of an abstract right determined a priori as a field subtracted from the rights of individuals, the Monarchomachic tradition exhausted the requirements of a liberal outlook. Prynne and Rutherford both drew their nourishment from this source, and the ideas of the Levellers rest upon a kindred foundation. Through Locke, it is at the base of the thought of Price and Priestley. Through Locke, also, it supplies the perspective of the American Revolution. Locke himself derived the substance of his ideas from the French thinkers of the Counter-Reformation. He drew upon Grotius and Puffendorf, who are, in turn, dependent upon the Monarchomachic school. The other great formative influence in Locke is Hooker's Ecclesiastical Polity; and if its eighth book is an attempt at refutation of the Vindiciae, that is itself sufficient to show that it is an essential source of early English radicalism.

After Rousseau, the situation changes because the foundation of political thought is different. That new theories had been born did not, of course, involve the disappearance of the tradition embodied in the Vindiciae, but it involved its transformation to new purposes. For the Social Contract introduces the notion of an organic state. The rights of the individual are superseded by the theory of corporate personality. That revival of Platonist doctrine was, in the long run, a death-blow to the atomism of the earlier school. It made the state not, as with the Vindiciae, the artificial contrivance of men, but a society which supplied human nature with its essential penumbra. If Rousseau lays excessive emphasis upon the degree to which man must be read in a state-context, that was the natural reaction from the individualism of Locke.

Nor was Rousseau the only corrective that outlook was to receive. With Hume and Bentham theories of abstract right gave place to theories of concrete utility, and the idea of a social contract did not survive the assault they made upon it. The discovery Bentham owed to Holbach that the creative power of the state lies in legislation — a theory built upon the Esprit des Lois — added a substance to the theory of politics which had been previously absent. For legislation meant the possibility of deliberate innovation, and that nation was qualitatively different from the declaration of a priori rightness which lies at the bottom of Monarchomachic doctrine. Utilitarianism, in brief, brought in the time-spirit as the permanent and conscious background of political philosophy. There is a chasm which cannot be bridged between rights regarded as the product of utility, and rights, as with the Vindiciae, that have their basis in an eternal right which escapes the categories of space and time.

This does not, indeed, mean that the Monarchomachs were mistaken in the perception their work enshrines. At the bottom of their argument is an emphasis which no political philosophy can afford to neglect. In part, it is the realisation that every state is built upon the consciences of men. Within each individual mind there are reserves into which no organising power can hope to penetrate. For the Vindiciae those reserves were, from the nature of its problem, mainly religious in nature, but the concept is a general one, and it applies to the spiritual outlook of every citizen. In part, also, it is the insistence that the state exists to secure for its members some agreed minimum of civilisation. Wherein that minimum consists will, of course, depend upon the character of each age. What only is certain is that the deprivation of certain things deemed good, will, at some given time, lead to the onset of resistance. Natural rights and a social contract raise, as historic concepts, far more difficulties than they solve. But it is important to bear in mind that they are, at the same time, the reflection of ideas upon which the successful working of every state depends.

They are the attempt, in fact, of men who feel that they are being deprived of that which gives to social life its meaning, to insist upon the remedy of their grievance. The social contract is an effort to provide such an institutional channel as will secure that the consent of the mass, and not the arbitrary will of a few, is the creative factor in the making of social tradition. Natural rights are the demands for the fulfilment of certain conditions without which an important fragment of the state ceases to feel loyalty to its institutions. However we phrase their substance, an answer to the problems they raise is integral to an adequate political philosophy. Nor may we neglect the important sense in which even the atomism of this outlook has its value. For to whatever degree society may absorb its members, it is, in their experience, ultimately interstitial in character. No theory of the state is satisfactory which does not realise that man is a solitary creature not less than social. The problem of allegiance is, therefore, in any final analyses, an individual problem. The law may resolve, and attach sanctions to its resolution, but the decision that is made takes place, if it is a real decision, separately in the mind of each member of the state. This has, of course, been seen by all men who have, at periods of crisis, been driven to challenge the foundations of a social system. It was true of Luther, it was true of Lamennais, of Dollinger and of Tyrrell. Perhaps, indeed, no better test of institutional adequacy can be found than the degree in which it leaves room for the free play of conscience, for no world is worth preserving which cannot utilise its Athanasius. Some such conclusion as this is, it is clear, implied in the experience of the sixteenth century. At that time the conscience involved, the rights demanded, were mainly religious in texture. Yet it is rather the emphasis than the nature of the problem that has shifted. The reconciliation of authority with freedom, the decision as to what things a creative freedom must embody, are not less pressing in our century than they were at the time of the Reformation.

V

The authorship of the Vindiciae has been for three centuries a matter of learned dispute; and it cannot be said that any certainty has been attained in the matter. Until the publication of Bayle's article in the Dictionnaire Critique, it was usual to assume that Duplessis-Mornay, the counsellor of Henry IV, was its author, though other attributions, most notably that to Theodore Beza, were not wanting. The latter, indeed, was a very popular theory with English royalist writers of the seventeenth century, since it afforded additional evidence of the natural and inherent disloyalty of the Presbyterians. Bayle did not, indeed, state definitely that Languet was the author of the Vindiciae, but he constructed an able and impressive case against any other attribution. He pointed out that Agrippa d'Aubigné, a contemporary witness, definitely states that Languet was the author; and that where, in his first edition of 1616, he had been discreet, in the second there is simple affirmation. He quotes also a supposed remark of Goulart, an indefatigable controversialist of the time, to the effect that the work was Languet's, but this testimony is weakened by the fact that the remark does not come directly from Goulart, but is attributed to him by Tronchin, the author of his funeral sermon. He points out, further, that if Duplessis-Mornay was the author of the book, he wrote at an early age an essay of remarkable ability.

The implication being that its composition seems more suited to the maturity of Languet. Bayle certainly destroys any other possibility than the alternative between Languet and his younger friend. He shows clearly that there is no basis whatever for the belief that the Vindiciae was due to Beza, or Hotman, or, as an English tradition suggested, the Jesuit Robert Parsons. This last theory, indeed, can only be based upon the assumption that as Parsons wrote many books anonymously attacking legitimate Kingship, the Vindiciae might reasonably be laid also to his charge.

Bayle's tentative view held the field for nearly two centuries. At the end of that time the theory that Duplessis-Mornay was the real author was urged independently both in France and Germany. It was impossible to deny the positive statement of d'Aubigné. There was the remark of Grotius, who, as Bayle says, "knew almost all that passed in the republic of letters," on the other side. Even d'Aubigné's positive assertion is not beyond doubt, for in the first edition of his work he had ascribed to "a learned gentleman of the Kingdom," a phrase much more applicable to Duplessis-Mornay, who was a French subject, than to Languet, who was the servant of a foreign sovereign. There are, moreover, two pieces of testimony which go to outweigh any other evidence we have. The Academician Conrart knew an acquaintance of Duplessis-Mornay. The latter, it appears, kept among his books a cabinet in which his own writings were preserved, and the friend had seen the Vindiciae among those writings. This can, at the least, be set against the supposed witness of Goulart. As M. Waddington urges, it is difficult to escape the implications of an express statement of Madame Duplessis-Mornay. She wrote her reminiscences, as she tells us, that her son might know what manner of man his father was, and, if her Protestantism is ardent, the value of her evidence is beyond all question. She writes that her husband was the author of an essay on la puissance légitime d'un prince sur son peuple, which is practically the title of the translation of the Vindiciae issued in French in 1581. There is no other work of Duplessis-Mornay's to which this can refer. There was no special point, at the time when Madame Duplessis-Mornay prepared her reminiscences, in claiming authorship for her husband, rather, in the circumstances of the period, it was an invitation to calumny if she intended her work to be published. If, still more, she wrote only for the eyes of her son, it is even clearer that she had no motive in not telling the truth. Until, then, evidence of equal weight be produced upon the other side, the balance of probability would appear to lean decisively towards the authorship of Duplessis-Mornay.

Nor can there be any doubt of his literary capacity for the work. His theological writing apart, his statesmanlike insight into the problems of his time made him, Sully apart, the most trusted of Henry IV's advisers. His ability to write under an aspect not his own is shown by his Exhortation à la Paix of 1574, written as an appeal by a moderate Catholic to his co-religionists; and his Remonstrance aux Estats of 1576, a plea to the Estates of Blois for peace, was published under a similar guise. He may, indeed, almost be called the professional advocate of Henry IV. If the tone of the Vindiciae is markedly different from his other writings, it may be suggested that, theology apart, it was the only essay addressed to the Huguenots, and the only one in which his effort was rather to encourage his friends than to persuade his opponents. Evidence of style is notoriously deceptive, but the stern eloquence of the Vindiciae seems to fit, not merely his other polemical works, but also the rugged severity of his character. Nor is it worthless to note that, like much else of his work, the Vindiciae displays in quotation a profound acquaintance with Scripture. That is a trait markedly absent from the writings of Languet. The latter's polished Latinity is very different from the simplicity of the Vindiciae's diction.

The English translation was published in London by Robert Baldwin in 1689. It is an anonymous translation, and appears to be an exact reproduction of an earlier one published in the not less significant year of 1648. Its Latin dress apart, indeed, the Vindiciae has a fairly consecutive English history which bears testimony to the favour with which it was received. It was printed entire in 1581 and 1589. In 1588 the fourth question appeared separately as A short Apologie for Christian Soldiers — obviously as a defence of English assistance to the Dutch rebels. A translation appeared in 1622, and a reprint of 1631 appears as Vindiciae Religionis, perhaps as an invitation to English Puritans to throw off the yoke of Stuart despotism. There were further editions in 1648, 1660, and 1689. In a century, that is, the Vindiciae was reprinted, either in whole or in part, no less than eight times; and each year of its appearance has a special import directly related to its text. No translator of any of these editions is known. Yet it is perhaps a service due to a picturesque legend to note that the copy in the British Museum of the edition of 1648 attributes the work to one William Walker of Darnel, near Sheffield, who cut off the head of Charles I. The anonymous commentator was perhaps drawing upon a fervid imagination, but the destruction of the Stuarts was not unconnected to the Vindiciae contra Tyrannos.

2

THE REALM OF EVENTS

In the centuries' unchallenged view of Polybius is first his recognition of the then accepted position that the state has three political systems, monarchy, aristocracy and democracy. Once accepted, Polybius goes on to reconstruct it. Observing that these are not fixed in character, monarchies behaving like tyrannies, aristocracies behaving badly, and democracies abandoning civil values. What Polybius then proposed was a more dynamic model which had in it an inner implied and cyclical view of human societies. Polybius perceived six types of constitution. In what he calls the natural and spontaneous course of events, the first system to emerge is monarchy moving from primitive leadership to kingship. Monarchy degenerates into tyranny which in turn gives way to aristocracy. The rule of the few becomes corrupted into an oligarchy. It rouses the masses into resisting injustices, giving rise to democracy. The democracy far from being a completion of flux leads inevitably to the breaking of laws, and ultimately, mob rule, and that brings the cycle to an end.

Once leadership is established the masses preserve his rule and make sure it is passed down to his descendants in view that those born to kings and reared by them will hold to the principles of the family. There followed security from the king and provision for his people in fortified castles, then as time passed, tyranny took over as a means of assuring safety.

Tyranny was seen as displeasing by the highest ranking of families and they acted in consort to protect themselves from being treated like the masses. This brought aristocracy to the fore. As time eroded their noble behaviour they descended to a decadence and greed that reduced them to an oligarchy. Its excesses drove the people to rebellion and they forced a new ruleship of legal responsibility and just administration. Democracy, the last phase in turn abandoned its values and moral clarity. The end result, a mob rule – calling out for a strong leader.

It is not possible to survey the movement of human society through its cyclical changes as analysed by Polybius without at the same time being aware that, so distinctly different are they, each phase of the cycle will produce different kinds of men. As we distinguish the clan moving to kingship, so we observe the closed society of an aristocracy, the fear of the masses under tyranny, and the low quality of manhood chosen as a reflection of a mass franchise.

In order to gauge just how profound these human evaluations are when formed and how they mutate through the dynamics of societal patterning, let us note the emergence from clan identity to the call for kingship. After that, can be noted the character of monarchy in identifying its need to honour its people. Here firstly is a brilliant translation of the Gaelic battle call of a Highland clan by a fellow alumnus of my old school, its motto being appropriately, 'Respice Prospice.' In this call can be seen that point at which tribal society has so evolved that it is able to define a vision of a king among men.

CLAN DONALD'S CALL
TO BATTLE AT HARLAW

After the Gaelic of Lachlann Mór Mac-Mhuirich (fl 1411)

You Clan of Conn remember this:
Strength from the eye of the storm.
Be at them, be animals,
Be alphas, be Argus-eyed,
Be belters, be brandishers,
Be bonny, be batterers,
Be cool heads, be caterans,
Be clashers, be conquerors,
Be doers, be dangerous,
Be dashing, be diligent,
Be eager, be excellent,
Be eagles, be elegant,
Be foxy, be ferrety,
Be fervid, be furious,
Be grimmer, be gralloching,
Be grinders, be gallopers,
Be hardmen, be hurries,
Be hell-bent, be harriers,
Be itching, be irritants,
Be impish, be infinite,

Be lucky, be limitless,
Be lashers, be loftiest,
Be manly, be murderous,
Be martial, be militant,
Be noxious, be noisiest,
Be knightly, be niftiest,
Be on guard, be orderly,
Be off now, be obdurate,
Be prancing, be panic-free,
Be princely, be passionate,
Be rampant, be renderers,
Be regal, be roaring boys,
Be surefire, be Somerleds,
Be surgers, be sunderers,
Be towering, be tactical,
Be tip-top, be targetters,
Be urgent, be up for it,
In vying be vigorous,
In ending all enemies.
Today is for triumphing,
You hardy great hunting-dogs,
You big-boned braw battle boys,
You lightfoot spry lionhearts,
You wall of wild warriors,
You veterans of victories,

You heroes in your hundreds here,
You Clan of Conn, remember this:
Strength from the eye of the storm.

ROBERT CRAWFORD

Kingship, that identified character of a man, making him worthy of ruling over others, set out parameters, the necessary parameters of monarchy. Monarchy in its fullest manifestation represented not only a ruler of capacity in office but a continuity of the rule by heredity. Seen from outside its system this suggests that ruling was being considered as belonging to a man and by extension his descendants. This is itself a distortion of a complex and functioning pattern in society that formed the arterial system of alliances, war and gentry across national borders. Births, deaths and marriages were the dynamic forces of civic society thus from the heights of wealth to the extent of lands, every stage of the way was manifested by personal bonds, everything that was in society had a human face.

The reformation that emerged in Europe was ideological and dominated by the political teachers, Luther and Calvin. In England where the deep break between wealth and land possession which forced Rome out of the nation, manifested to the people as a rejected, childless catholic woman, a King determined to complete his monarchic task with an inheritor, a gentry in conflict over royal ties to possible brides, in short a human web of ambitions, power and change.

Heredity as a genealogical tree system made sense since it was based on risking the success of genetic couplings from among families reared to rule. Its flaw was twofold. One if the direct line produced an anomalous, i.e. unkingly creature, and two if the line ceded to the branch which in turn produced a failure. The Wars of the Roses showed the waste of a battle to sustain the line, while its ending produced England's greatest monarch, Henry VIII. The Julio-Claudian line of Rome ended in the disastrous cousinage that produced Claudius, Caligula and Nero! In the Polybius view, the end of monarchy, its senescence, is tyranny.

It must not be forgotten while recording the failures among the monarchs that it has its basis in capacity and a creature with a sense of statecraft.

Look at the poem the young King Henry wrote to his bride, Mary Queen of Scots. Buried under centuries of catholic slander which required him to be disastrous in order that his wife could emerge as a catholic martyr, there can now be discerned a gifted young man with all the potentials of monarchy. Genetically an heir of two kingdoms, raised to be king of one of them, he impatiently took the way of marriage and fatally married the homeless Mary Stewart. As she hurtled to her doom she managed to plot her unfortunate husband's end as well. Young King Henry was assassinated, aged twenty-two. If his wife had responded to his guidance in his poem her story might have been different. She could not see who he was much less her own destiny.

HENRY STUART, KING OF SCOTS

1545-1567
To the Queen

Be governour baith guid and gratious;
Be leill and luifand to thy liegis all;
Be large of fredome and no thing desyrous;
Be just to pure for one thing may fall;
Be ferme of faith and constant as ane wall;
Be reddye evir to stanche evill discord;
Be cheretabill, and sickerlye thou sall
Be bowsum ay to knaw thy God and Lord.

Be nocht to proud of wardlie guidis heir;
Be well bethocht thai will remane na tyde;
Be sicker als that thou man die but weir;
Be war thairwith the tyme will no man byde;
Be vertewus and set all vyce on syde;
Be patient, lawlie and misericord;
Be rewlit so quhairevir thou go or byde;
Be bowsum ay to knaw thy God and Lord.

Be weil avysit of quhome thow cousale tais;
Be sewer of thame that thai be leill and trew;
Bethink the als quhidder thai be freindis, or fais.
Be to thy saull, thair sawis or thou persew:
Be nevir our hastye to wirk and syne to rew;
Be nocht their freind that makis the fals record;
Be reddye evir all guid workis to renew;
Be bowsum ay to knaw thy God and Lord.

Be traist and conquese thy awin heritage
Be ennemyes of auld now occupyit;
Be strenth and force thou sobir thai man swage
Be law of God – thair may no man deny it;
Be nocht as lantern in mirknes unspyit;
Be thou in rycht thi landis suld be restored,
Be wirschop so thy name beis magnefeit;
Be bowsum ay to knaw thy God and Lord.

Be to rebellis strong as lyoun eik;
Be ferce to follow thame quhairevir thai found;
Be to thy liegemen bayth soft and meik;
Be thair succor and help thame haill and sound;
Be knaw thy cure and caus quhy thow was cround;
Be besye evir that justice be nocht smord;
Be blyith in hart; thir wordis oft expound;
Be bowsum ay to knaw thy God and Lord.

pure: the poor folk	sickerlye: surely	bowsum: tractable
guidis: goods	sicker: sure	man: must
weir: doubt	sawis: words	wirk: act
Swage: assuage	eik: each, any	smord: smothered

The dismal modernist imposition of the democratic idea as synonymous with a universal franchise has overshadowed the other profound change that separates the modern from the prior mode of governance. The revolutionist view that government by the people is superior to government by an elite or an individual covers over the change which, in deep, marks the crisis now engulfing the failure of the evolutionist view. Not realising what that change was precluded a renewal of the social nexus.

The change was defined by Trotsky. He intended a future which not only did without rulers but effectively negated the ruled, for that latter reality implied that from them a ruler might emerge. Trotsky commanded: 'Replace the government of men with the administration of things.' The great Malaparte had made his crucial distinction in 'Technique of the Coup d'Etat' when he had defined Lenin as the State and Trotsky as the revolution. He saw that the latter intended the abolition of the former. Stalin, posing as Leninist had applied the revolutionary doctrine, that is Trotsky's, but maintaining the claimed truth that a new state had been founded. We had entered the modern world. This doctrine produced both the concentration camp and the gulag as instruments of slave labour. It equally rationalised the elimination of the class enemy or the race enemy. It licenced the obliteration of enemy cities, Berlin, Hamburg, Dresden, the Rhur cities, Hiroshima and Nagasaki.

This new foundational doctrine of the modern techno-world by its implementation in eliminating men from the process, eliminated or insisted on eliminating the activating human self and its psyche, and therefore by extension its existential and its inherited memory, in short its very D.N.A. as record.

The result of this meant that an examination of process, historical or political, in the end had to submit to a now absolutist utilitarian and pragmatic evaluation. With the ancient Jewish and Muslim understanding of one sovereign Lord of the creation and its harmonic running of nature without representational form or identity, with that eliminated and god in turn reduced to idea, the understanding of the human situation was reduced to a dynamic, utterly controlled unit, acting and reacting among the other myriad things.

Political discourse and the very possibility of even mentioning liberty was reduced to the formulation of slogans. Declarations of independence, rights, constitutions, all speech was encompassed by the command of Trotsky.

Only metaphor and imagined narrative became possible. From Aristotle to Rousseau the discourse of governance is shunted into a platform of the station without exit.

In the desert of modernity all that remains are the broken statues of warning by Orwell, '1984' and 'Animal Farm' leaving to the explorers to reach Marlowe on to Seneca's tragedies, Lucan's epic, and Ovid's 'Metamorphoses'.

Once it has been grasped that a society changes through the faces of the Polybius model man himself changes, so also in evidence of this it can be seen that language changes. Language is the instrument of truth-telling but it can also devolve – not into lie-telling, but something much more dangerous – fiction-telling, the narration to other men of a view that in itself precludes the liberating action.

Thus Thucydides in his 'History of the Peloponnesian War' in analysing the effects of civil war and anarchy indicates the impact social crises had on men. 'They reversed the usual evaluative force of words to suit their own assessment of actions.'

It follows that the identity of a governing body free to confront issues without fear is not simply a structural matter. Not only must that body be unrestrained in its judgments but it already necessitates a personnel trained and equipped to mutual discourse, in short trained to a mode of speech that will move its listeners. Such a senate requires not only senators but a shared rhetoric between its members.

In the 'Vindiciae contra Tyrannos' it states: 'But Rome is there, according to the saying of Pompey, where the Senate is, and the Senate is where there is obedience to the Laws. Love of liberty, and studious carefulness for the country's preservation.'

Cicero's great series of speeches in confrontation with Mark Antony he named his Philippics (Orationes Philippicae) in deliberate echo of Demosthenes' Philippic Orations which were made by the Greek orator attacking King Philip II of Macedon. Cicero used this title on sending the text to Brutus who admired Demosthenes and himself aspired to the Attic school of rhetoric.

Classicists use the term 'rhetoric of crisis.' Ramsey and Manuwald define it as 'not simply produced by external circumstances, but in part brought into being by Cicero's portrayal of certain events as threatening and calling for an immediate response.' Thus the orator among his fellow senators is confronting external crises and by the instruments of governance, its proponents, and an applied linguistic method, these same men from being passive receptors of civic events are transformed into free men choosing their destiny without any restraining fear. This is liberty.

In Pompey's phrase 'where the Senate is' means the location, the men and among them Cicero using a language of both style and structure, a rhetoric, and rhetoric as spoken by an orator which rouses these men, that Senate, from dream to reality, from passivity to action, that is to resistance which itself is freedom. Here is Cicero both aligning himself with Caesar's assassins and exposing Mark Antony as the in depth enemy of the Republic.

Reliquorum quam velis esse causam; edormi crapu-
lam, inquam, et exhala. An faces admovendae sunt
quae excitent tantae causae indormentem? Mum-
quamne intelleges statuendum tibi esse utrum illi qui
istam rem cesserunt homicidaene sint an vindices
liberatis?

(Cicero: Phillipic 2. 30)

'Rouse yourself from your intoxication, I say, and
blow it all out. Will it take lighted torches to rouse
you from your slumbers over an issue like this? (He
is addressing Mark Antony before the Senate) Will
you never understand that you have to make up your
mind whether the authors of that deed (Caesar's
murder) are murderers or champions of freedom?'

So, by the use of his rhetorical technique, in the delivery of an
expert orator, Cicero both casts out the presence of Mark Antony
from among the Republicans and at the same time seals the unity
of the Senate in support of the conspirators.

The condition of liberty enshrined in the capacity to exchange
conflicting views in open discourse without fear of punishment
is not only a fragile achievement only briefly sustained, but it in
turn is something that emerges uniquely at a time when all these
givens are possible and that is determined within a moving cycle
of events vibrating between dictatorship and anarchy.

The emergence of such a body – upholding law, creating laws,
and commanding policy – does not happen on the instant. Prior
civil conditions must first emerge and later be developed to that
point where the granting of power to a body of men may be
activated.

In our primal Republic the order of events is clearly outlined. It begins with the first King setting out the pattern of civic life.

> 'Rebus divinis rite perpetratis vocataque ad concilium multitudine, quae coalescere in populi unius corpus nulla re praeterquam legibus poterat, iura dedit.'
>
> (Livy I. viii. I.)

> 'When Romulus had duly attended to the worship of the gods, he called the people together and gave them the rules of law, since nothing else but law could unite them into a single body politic.'

He then appointed twelve lictors who carried axes in bundles of rods in readiness to carry out the law in scourging and decapitation. This confirmed the monarchic rule of law.

> The next stage followed.
> 'Cum iam virium haud paeniteret, consilium deinde viribus parat. Centum creat senatores, sive quia is numerous satis erat, sive quia soli centum erant qui creari patres possent. Patres certe at honore, patriciique progrenies eorum appellati.'
>
> (Livy I. viii. 7)

> 'He now had no reason to be dissatisfied with his strength, and proceeded to add policy to strength. He appointed a hundred senators, whether because this number seemed to him enough, or because there were no more than a hundred who could be designated fathers. At all events they received the

designation of fathers from their rank, and their descendants were called patricians.'

The natural mark of the beginning of a state, as opposed to a tribe, is its expansion.

'Roma interim crescit Albae ruinis.'

(Livy: I. xxx. I.)

'Rome, meanwhile, was increased by Alba's downfall.'

Monarchy, as in the model of Polybius, eventually fell into decadence. The moral order, established originally by the first King was corrupted. The fasces upheld the power of the law for the people but now the royal family saw itself as above that same law. That same corrupted family had among them the son of Tarquinia, sister of the King. He was a man of a different calibre. Having learned that leading men of the state, including his own brother, had been put to death by his uncle, he adopted the role of a fool, even accepting the name of stupidity itself – Brutus. Behind that name was the man who would create the Republic and free the Romans, Lucius Junius Brutus.

On a royal visit to Delphi, the young men decided to ask the Oracle which one of them should be king at Rome. The answer came that the highest power in Rome would go to the first of the young men to kiss his mother. They all determined to rush back to Rome secretly so that one of them could fulfill the decree. Brutus knew to interpret the Pythian wisdom. Pretending to stumble, he fell and touched his lips to the earth, as the common mother of all mortals.

On his return to Rome he landed into the crisis of the rape of Lucretia by Sextus Tarquinius. The outrage was climaxed by her suicide. Livy recounts the historical aftermath.

> 'Brutus illis luctu occupatis cultrum ex volnere Lucretiae extractum manantem cruore praese tenens, "Per hunc," inquit, "castissimum ante regiam iniuriam sanguinem iuro, vosque, di, testes facio me L. Tarquinium Superbum cum scelerata coniuge et omni liberorum stirpe ferro, igni quacumque denique vi possim, executurum nec illos nec alium quemquam regnare Romae passurum.'
>
> (Livy I. lix. I.)

> "Brutus, while the others were absorbed in grief, drew out the knife from Lucretia's wound, and holding it up, dripping with gore, exclaimed: 'By this blood, most chaste until a prince wronged it, I swear, and I take you gods to witness, that I will pursue Lucius Tarquinius Superbus and his wicked wife and all his children, with sword and fire, aye, with whatsoever violence I may; and that I will suffer neither them nor any other to be king in Rome."

The sequence of events must be examined with care, for embedded in this narration is not only the event of the transition from monarchy to republic, but underneath it is the driving motor of one man awakening, responding and then initiating action.

At the beginning of the matter there is a patrician out of harmony with the power regime of the Tarquins. His adoption of the role of idiot not only indicates his awakened sense of survival but of his assuming in his person a conscious rebellion.

At Delphi, two things happen. In the first, the young men openly aspire and conspire. It is a covert move to power. In the second, Brutus steps forward and lays the claim to power. On kissing the earth Brutus has made his choice. The affair now rests with him – but he had decided on kingship.

At the house of Lucretia the transformative event for Brutus occurs. In the violence of the crime and the outrage of Brutus, a new moral imperative is born.

Born of a long resentment and a sudden insight, not only Tarquin the King is removed but kingship itself. Not power, not even personal power but the machine of monarchy is destroyed. In its place the new power individual installs a new machine. It has two principles: one, it is not a hereditary mechanism and two it is a short term mechanism. Thus two men will have power together, but one in active command. They in turn will be recycled among a limited patrician elite, the Senate. Brutus immediately raised the Senate to 300. Of the two ruling consuls, only one of them could hold the fasces (rods) of command. Thus, ruling power was transformed. It was not diminished, but it was de-geneticised and set time limits.

Livy confirms the matter.

'Libertatis antem originem inde magis quia annuum imperium consulare factum est quam quod dem- inutum quicquam sit ex regia potestate, numeres.'
(Livy II. i. 7)

"You may reckon the beginning of liberty as pro- ceeding rather from the limitation of the consul's authority to a year than from any diminution of the power compared with that which the kings had exercised."

This permits us to summarise the ultimately evolved form of governance called Republic and the limits set on power as a result.

Kingship and kings arrived at by genetic continuity are exiled. That power which adhered to both monarch and the monarchy becomes transferred. The patrician body of wealth and power invests two of its kind as proconsuls. Of the two, one will bear the fasces which symbolise the authority to punish and execute (that is by rod and axe). Their tenure as rulers lasts only one year. Interest is set as 1% and bankruptcy punished even by death. Finance as a road to power is thus barred.

It follows that the identity of the Senate conceals the instrument of liberty.

The common factor of the senatorial class was dual. They were patrician and rich, and they were bonded to military service and colonial governance.

The Senate represented a ruling elite which not only dispensed justice (the fasces), upholding the law, defining it and executing it, but, and this is what gave power to Rome, were its active military and governing force. It was this unified state that lasted hundreds of years. Men who defend a society with their lives implies a different kind of society from one where a section rule and another section give their lives for it.

This permits the conclusion that a mass-franchised society, where its rulers stay safely home and command the military operation carried out by an obedient army and generals, is diametrically opposed to the Republican society.

President Lincoln told General Ulysses S. Grant at their first private meeting, "All I had wanted, and had ever wanted, was someone who would take the responsibility and act." (Keegan: The Mask of Command 1987)

It follows that somewhere between Washington and Lincoln the concept of a political leader who was himself a soldier, unifying the two roles as Commander-in-Chief, was shattered. By the end of World War Two America has a President who orders the nuclear devastation of Hiroshima and Nagasaki and completes the political lesion of governance from the military by dismissing and humiliating America's greatest General, MacArthur. In sacking him the country was obliged by political means to accept a great nation in Asia being divided in two and plunging one half into ruthless Stalinism and a nuclear arms programme.

By the end of the century a President with two wars raging received the Nobel Peace Prize, and proceeded to sack his brilliant soldier, General McChrystal after admitting the military leader intimidated him.

Just as the primary condition of a functioning Senate upholding the law is a trained rhetorical body of law-givers, so a further necessary condition is that those who govern can themselves attack and defend.

The macabre mass slaughter of two world wars could never have happened if its perpetrators had had to suffer the blood, sweat and tears they boasted of, nor if its generals had not been prevented from command.

The disaster of political leaders playing at being generals, which is the dominant reality of the twentieth century slaughter-house, is no more dramatically to be found than in the dismal saga of Winston Churchill posing as War-Leader while theoretically a democratic Prime Minister.

The leading military historian Correlli Barnett is categoric. "By an amazing injustice … he blamed the collapse of O'Connor's conquests not on himself for his decision over Greece, but on Wavell. … There was no valid cause for relieving Wavell. In his two years in the Middle East he had built a base and a command structure from nothing. He had conquered the whole of Italian East Africa, and captured two hundred thousand prisoners, including the Duke of Aosta, Viceroy of Ethiopia. Under his strategic aegis, O'Connor had taken Cyrenaica and another two hundred thousand prisoners. Between February and June 1941 he had conducted six major campaigns, never less than three at a time, and in May five at a time. No other British soldier had the strategic grasp, the sagacity, the cool nerves and the immense power of leadership to do all these things and steer a course free of total disaster."

By 1942 the Churchill government was in crisis and lost a by-election by a colossal turnover of votes. Again it was time to sack another great general to deflect the blame from a collapse at the political core. This time it was the respected General Auchinleck. On August 3rd Churchill arrived in Cairo with Smuts to face the Commander-in-Chief, Middle East.

Correlli Barnett continues: "On the 4th also Wavell arrived from India; and the Prime Minister was able to play the role he loved, that of Marlborough, 'riding the whirlwind and directing the storm,' with Wavell, Auchinleck, Alan Brooke, Admiral Harwood, Tedder, Casey, the Minister of State, and Smuts.

"In the early morning of the 5th August, Auchinleck stood with his staff on the airstrip near 8th army headquarters and watched a figure in a siren suit and topee emerge from an aircraft into the white sunshine. For a moment they faced each other – the plump pink politician who ran the war from a cellar in London, and the lean, sun-dried soldier who had fought the battles."

Hitler, too, ran the war from his bunker in Berlin. From the hell of the Stalingrad Siege, his greatest General, Manstein, signalled to him, 'I am here. Where are you?'

The Republican model demands of its Senators a military and governing career as essential to the power elite.

Another necessary attribute is defined by Polybius.

"The Senate's most important role is that it controls the treasury, in the sense that it is responsible for all state revenues and almost all expenditure."

Ibn Khaldun basically confirms the Roman model of power as designed in its Republican phase.

"Power rests on two indispensible foundations: the first, which is the power and brotherhood (asabiyya) expressed in the army, the second is the money which upholds this and provides the needs of the state. When a state begins to collapse these two foundations start to go." (Muqaddima III, xlv. P624 Pleiade)

Ibn Khaldun goes on to define the two activities which mark a state's disintegration, luxury and along with it repression.

It follows from this discerned patterning that in the present world there is simply nothing that can offer itself as a Republic. Once the army is a privately paid and conscripted entity, once the financial is in the hands of corporate structures, it follows that the reality of the state, as such, has been dismantled.

Hobbes saw immediately that the growth of corporate self-governing structures entailed, step by step, the end of state power. With implacable logic he pointed out that corporation was itself modelled on the state and that at a certain point the corporations would render state structures irrelevant and therefore redundant. If the states in a final bid to survive set up super-state structures, as with the League of Nations then the United Nations, NATO, the continental versions, as in Europe and South America, they would only be checkmated by a similar bonding of discrete corporations on a global scale. The age of nations and joined nations was over.

It follows from this that substantive power has eluded the rational grasp and the activating discourse.

* * * * *

In the present situation the world finds itself, the first bitter truth dawns upon us. So radical has been the abandonment of previous, one might say classical models of state, it is almost assumed that there is no such thing. The universities, now governed under financial imperatives, no longer produce theoretical works which permit any profound critique of current power systems. Indeed for a work to appear under the imprimatur of a once respected university now immediately posed the critical question of its author's financial dependence.

Not since Laski's residence at the London School of Economics in the fifties as professor had a public voice directly examined the political foundations of the modern state. Today, to teach on fundamental issues of power and governance one has to seek in the literary byways of exclusive and often still privately funded colleges, Dartmouth, Cornell and Michigan and there can still be found relevant political thinking but it is deviously arrived at within the studies of Tacitus, Lucan and Marlowe.

The dominant myth governing all political thought now is that somehow, due to the superior thought-processes and higher critical methods, the masses of the French Revolution had finally ended individual rule and replaced it with social government.

They had thrown out the baby. Alas they had not thrown out the filthy bath water.

America was the first to pretend revolution. In fact it had been a coup d'état, and that by a General who claimed his life's meaning was based on Julius Caesar. The almost immediate result of the French Revolution forced the Americans to be clear about their political allegiance. This produced a profound split in the positions taken by the self-styled Founding Fathers, a title which directly admitted they were patrician, that is a superior elite.

However eloquent the discourse which launched the American state and despite its insistence on its Roman inheritance the emergent nation was founded on a fatal tripos.

Its first and dominant community was forged by a federal bonding over a vast territory of individual states with their own banks.

Its further community lay in the former slave population freed from bonded labour but simply never granted the founding citizenship and contract of the other settlers, the former slave owners.

Its hidden community the original Americans of the great tribes, once owners of the continent, then reduced to small reservations and the land itself expropriated by the new power system of the settlers.

At present Americans still prefer a guilty discourse of failure to grant equal status to the ex-slaves to the impossible admission that the whole democratic experiment is based on the stolen territory of the original American peoples, Navaho, Sioux, Chicasaw, Cherokee, Creek, Seminole, Apache, Cheyenne, Arapaho, Iroquois.

As for America's claim to be a Roman state in its fundamental role of Senate, the primordial necessity of Romanness, in America what began as a State product chosen by each state's legislature, thus giving a semblance of elite independence, was reduced to a body chosen by mass franchise and thus voided of its exclusive identity, both Houses being determined in the same manner.

Add to that the Nixonian change from a national army to a privately funded professional entity. In Ferguson's view a vital characteristic of Rome, was removed.

By the end of World War II, with American empire at its most extensive, and with the political frame already so compromised, an evolutionary growth of banking emerged alongside a corporation dominance of industry and commerce far beyond the social model of pre-war America.

The danger for modern society globally was that the link of supra-national corporation power to financial webbing left critical analysis of the state with an outdated philosophy and terminology. In the end all theoretical claims to just governance were abandoned, leaving the modern techno-peasants with a mere handful of slogans – democracy, tolerance, human rights and Wilson's mad doctrine of the right of self-determination (for a state!) which itself left millions dead.

When, at last, in 2014, a historian unravelled and decoded the causes of World War One in a brilliant narrative that made sense of what had been up till then a dualist fantasy of wicked Kaiser against kindly democrats, Christopher Clark's profound and detailed study 'The Sleepwalkers' was promptly dismissed as 'revisionist history', a sub-category of conspiracy theory, therefore to be ignored.

The failure to confront the present crisis was directly a result of having accepted philosophy as an instrument of political theory instead of narrative. It was Rousseau and Adam Smith who led to a system that transferred liberty from a group experience to a mathematically structured model of totalitarianism, that is world-empire.

Having established that liberty was itself the event of a small group of governance imposing law, unrestricted by force, and recognising it as an in-time phenomenon which in turn needs a language, a rhetoric and men of moral virtue, a further understanding is required to appreciate it fully and also see the forces that deny it and destroy it.

This demands, firstly, a glance at Caesar and secondly a mirror reflection of Ovid.

3

THE CAESAR FACTOR

Before we can arrive at a profound assessment of the act of tyrannicide which ended the dictator's life, and before, therefore, one can appreciate the assassins – all twenty three of them led by Cassius and Brutus, it should be clear what manner of man was Caesar.

Let us take Cicero as our guide to the senators who killed Caesar. Let us take Lucan, the great chronicler of 'The Civil War', written by a poet who was a victim of the Empire that emerged on the ruins of the Republic, as our guide to Caesar.

Having lived through a hideous century of continental military devastation and a set of dictators, half claiming totalitarian rule and the other half pretending to the service of parliament, it has to be set on record that the cult of Caesar has dominated the historical view.

Theodor Mommsen the renowned historian, wrote in 1856:

'...the historian, when once in a thousand years he encounters the perfect, can only be silent regarding it.'

In 1866 the militarily disastrous Napoleon III produced a serious 'Histoire de Jules Caesar' halted by his debacle in 1870, which also contained his more formidable uncle's History written on St. Helena.

The most trustworthy contemporary historian of Caesar is Luciano Canfora. Yet the work, entitled 'Giulio Caesar: il Dittatore Democratico' emerged from the University of California re-titled, 'Julius Caesar: the life and times of the People's Dictator.' American intellectuals could not handle the essential political truth discerned by the Italian scholar.

The brilliant student of Stefan George, Friedrich Gundolf made a study of the Caesar myth and model through the centuries, 'The Mantle of Caesar' proving how embedded in European historical thinking is the legendary reputation which transforms dictator into super-hero and as rescuer of the state from senatorially governed society.

The core of the dictator's identity does not lie in his record of terrible cruelty in Gaul, the genocide of thousands, cutting off the hands of conquered soldiers and most offensive of all his imprisonment, degradation and murder of Cingetorix, leader of the Treveri, a man he had called his friend!

There is one incident that makes clear the true nature of this man while in the process of taking over his whole epoch, and Rome itself.

It is the event of his return to Rome after the wars in Gaul. He headed for the Temple of Saturn which served as the Roman Treasury. Lucan describes the scene:

'Phoebea Palatia complet
Turba patrum nullo cogendi jure senatus
E latebris educta suis; non consule sacrae

Fulserunt sedes, non, proxima lege potestas,
Praetor adest, vacuaeque loco lessere curules.
Omnia Caesar erat: privatae curia vocis
                              Testis adest.' [III. 104-8]

'Authority to summon the Senate was wanting:
but a mob of Senators, brought out from their
hiding-places, filled the Temple of Apolus on the
Palatine; the splendour of the Consuls was absent
from their sacred seats; the praetors by law next
in office, were not in attendance, and the empty
chairs of office were removed from their places.
Caesar was all in all, and the Senate met to register
the utterance of a private man.'

Thus, in Lucan's view Caesar has rendered the Senate useless as an institution and done so before the renowned and in all probability the staged event of crossing the Rubicon.

Ferguson maintained that Caesar had determined on world power long before that declared point of inevitability.

Lucan goes on to show Caesar in his full identity as a man dictating events, controlling men and acquiring things.

Caesar backed by his army presented himself at the gates of the Temple of Saturn, Rome's treasury, and claimed for himself its wealth. In Lucan's phrase 'freedom broke out' when Metello stepped forward alone among the Senators to prevent robbery. Arrogantly Caesar had him pushed aside.

"Protinus abducto patuerunt temple Metello.
Tunc rupes Tarpeia sonat magnoque reclusas
Testator stridore fores; tum conditus imo

Eruitur temple multis non tactus ab annis
Romani census populi, quem Punica bella,
Quem dederat Perses, quem victim praeda Philippi,
Quod tibi, Roma, fuga Pyrrhus trepidante reliquit;
Quod te Fabricius regi non vendidit auro;
Quidquid parcorum mores servastis avorum;
Quod dites Asiae populi misère tributum,
Victorique dedit Minoia Creta Metello;
Quod Cato longinqusvexit super equora Cypro.
Tunc Orientis opes, captorumque ultima regum,
Quae Pompejanis praelata est, gaza, triumphis,
Egeritur: tristi spoliantur temple rapina;
Pauperiorque fuit tunc primum Caesare Roma."

[III. 153-168]

"Metellus was drawn aside and the Temple at once thrown open. Then the Tarpeian Rock re-echoed and long grating bore witness to the opening of the doors; then was brought forth the wealth of the Roman people, stored in the Temple vaults and untouched for many a year — treasure from the Punic wars and Perses, and the spoil of conquered Philip; the gold that the Gaul in his hasty flight forfeited to Rome, and the gold that could not bribe Fabricius to sell Rome to the king; all that the thrift of our ancestors saved up; all the tribute paid by the wealthy nations of Asia, and all that was handed over to conquering Metellus by Minoan Crete; and the store that Cato brought across the sea from distant Cyprus. Lastly, the riches of the East were brought to light, the far-fetched treasures of captive kings that was borne along in Pompey's triumph. Dismal was the deed of plunder that robbed the Temple; and then for the first time Rome was poorer than a Caesar."

In this event Caesar confirms the dual nature of political power. It needs an army and an army needs money. There lies beneath that a protocol which should not be spoken, for it reveals the enslavement of the masses, that is, to be precise once bereft of consultative command and openly applied justice. Again, it is Caesar with his army. He informs them according to Lucan, as follows:

'An vos momenta putatis
Ulla dedisse mihi? numquau sic cura deorum
Se premet, ut vestrae morti vestraeque salut,
Fata vacent; procerum motus haec cuncta secuntur:
Humanum paucis vivt genus.'

[Lucan. 5. 331-343]

'Think you that you have ever turned the scale in my favour? Providence will never stoop so low that fate can attend to the life and death of such as you. All these events depend upon the actions of the leaders: it is for the sake of a few that mankind lives.'

This view represents the end of discourse and thus cuts off the highest dimension of the human creature. It removes the understanding of colloquy, of people coming together and settling the civic affair.

Add to that world-view which removes – well, everybody, must be placed the recognition by Cicero, that master of the clear word and the blurred confirmation of the impossible others, that there was a dark other side to the ruling dictator. With that unfailing insight that had steered him through Rome's crises, he noted to Atticus that perhaps Caesar was unstoppably surging on to further, even endless battles. 'Caesar might never have returned.' 'Ille enim numquam revertisset.' [letters to Atticus: 15. 4. 3.]

Here, Cicero lays bare an inescapable element in the make-up of the dictator-conqueror. The plunging, urgent unstoppable nature of the creature, in this he was not in command. If he was the child of fortuna he was, in the end, the victim of fata.

Caesar's life was itself a hurtling, a precipitation. Urgency. His conquest of Gaul, his Civil War, his take over of the Roman Republic and the Ides of March – they were all rushed. The soothsayer warned him, 'Beware the Ides of March.' 'Look,' he retorted, 'it has come and I am still alive!' The man repeated, 'Yes, but it is not over yet.' And on he rushed to the Senate. The message warning of the planned assassination he brushed aside. Stabbed again and again, it was only on the wound of Brutus, at the last, he may finally have stopped to take in the existence of the other.

Now – the act of assassination.

In the days before the fatal encounter in the Senate from a list of disastrous decrees announced the beginnings of a lifelong dictatorship. Cicero was openly referring to him as Rex, the most hated term in Republican language.

An ivory statue on its litter was to be carried with the god's images to the Circus. A statue inscribed 'to the unconquerable god' was placed in the Temple of Quirinus. The ruler cult was being introduced into Rome by an acquiescent Senate, one already increased to 900. The Senate, in Matthias Gelzer's words had been turned into "a large and devoted imperial civil service."

On February 15 he officially took on the title of Dictator Perpetuus.

> 'At etian ascribe iussit in fastis ad Lupercalia
> C. Caesari, dictatori perpetuo.'
>
> [Cicero: Philippic 2. 87]

> 'He even gave orders that the following notation
> be added to the calendar beside the date of the
> Lupercalia: to Gaius Caesar, dictator for life.'

So on that fatal day he entered the Senate, an institution he had already abolished. In the account of Suetonius when Brutus lashed at him with his dagger he exclaimed in Greek, 'You too, my child!' This gives a vibrancy to the long-rumoured story that Brutus was his child by Servilia who was known to have long nursed a passion for Caesar against all the political views of the men around Brutus and against her brother, Cato. According to Plutarch, 'Brutus gave him one blow in the groin.'

While it seems most unlikely that Caesar was his father there can be no denying who he was to his mother. In the light of this one has to note that the Republic was born by his ancestor, Lucius Junius Brutus who had permitted the execution of his two sons to preserve the new state. In this way the Republic could be said to have been born on the murder of the sons and to have died on the murder of the father.

It is in the most renowned of Cicero's Philippics, the second, that Cicero sets down the political principle underlying the murder of Julius Caesar. This complete document is the record and validation of the tyrannicide. Almost all the historians, rulers and writers get it wrong, but Cicero had set down the profound meaning of the event.

'At quem ad modum me coarguerit homo acutus recordamini. "Caesare interfecto" inquit "statim cruentum alte extollens Brutus pugionem Ciceronem nominatim exclamavit atque ei Recuperatam libertatem est gratulatus." cur mihi potissimum?'

[Cicero Phil. 2. 28]

'However, do remember how the clever fellow proved his point against me. "The moment Caesar was killed," says he, "Brutus raised his bloodstained dagger high, called on Cicero, by name and congratulated him on the recovery of freedom." Now why me in particular?'

Cicero goes further.

'Omnes ergo in culpa. Etenim omnes boni, quantum in ipsis fuit, Ceasarum occiderunt; aliis consilium, aliis animus, aliis occasio defuit; voluntatas nemini.'

[Cicero Phil. 2. 28]

'So we are all guilty. And so, all decent men killed Caesar so far as it was in them to do so: some lacked design, some courage, some opportunity; none lacked the will.'

Remember, that here Cicero is reminding the Senate that this is the matter of the Senate in its entirety, and one with consequences for future ages.

'Quae enim res umquam, pro sancte Iuppiter, non modo in hac urbe, sed in omnibus terris est gesta

maior, quae gloriosior, quae commendatior homi-
num memoriae ersempiternae.'

[Cicero Phil. 2. 32]

'For never, holy Jupiter, was a greater deed done in
Rome or anywhere else in the world, none more glorious, none more sure to live forever in the memory
of mankind.'

Cicero is in no doubt about the importance of this event not just
there, in Rome, but for the future ages of man.

'Quae vero tam immemor posteritas, quae tam
ingratae litterae reperiuntur quae eorum gloriam
non immortalitatis memoria prosequantua?'

[Cicero. Phil. 2. 33]

'No future age will be found so unmindful, no literature so ungrateful as not to preserve their glory
in everlasting remembrance.'

In the last phase of this part of the Second Philippic he adds a
comment which removes any doubt about why Caesar had to
be removed. If he had had a direct hand in the matter he would
also have had Anthony murdered. 'Non solum regem sed etiam
regnum de re publica sustulissem', removing not merely the monarch from the Republic but monarchy itself.

Brutus, Cassius and the Senators were not removing a dictator.
They had known others before Caesar. Brutus' conspiracy was
designed – not even to save the Senate, for it was already past
saving – but to set down in blood that the Republic founded by
his ancestors and now at its end, was the unique, utterly evolved

model to bring men together in consultation, justice, and moral quality outside the power of compulsion.

The Assassination Issue

Once the profound and permanent issue of the Brutus affair is recognised it obliges the issue of assassination as a political move on the board to be re-thought. The Augustus principate, so called by him, and Empire by history, then immediately reveals itself as a deception. The Tacitean view takes precedence over the now popular view of state dominance permanently out of reach of a manipulated electorate. After Augustus no-one ever is given a say in the doctrines of power, and that is true of the dictatorships posing as popular and the democracies comfortably ruled by a mere handful fronting for a chosen leader.

Yet from the post-Augustus age up until now the assassination issue is both proposed and sometimes imposed on the body politic as some kind of solution.

Look at the positive wave of assassinations that swept over the French body politic at the time of the crisis that climaxed in the St. Bartholomew's Day Massacre.

In 1562 Francois Duc de Guise was assassinated.

In 1572 occurred the terrible Massacre of St. Bartholomew's Day.

In 1588, Henri Duc de Guise was assassinated.

In 1589 Henry III was assassinated.

In 1610 Henri IV was assassinated although through him came what looked like a solution with his ordering of the Edict of Nantes.

Behind the dramatis personae of that troubled epoch lay the unfolding dreams of the dying universalist, or global, system of The Catholic Church, faced with the emergence of the Reformation, that is to say the replacement of a centralised command system from Rome with the individually chosen doctrine of belief free of the mystical 'hic est corpus' which, when operated by licensed priests turned wine into the actual blood of Christ.

As Laski with genius has analysed the political issues facing France at the time of the clash between global catholicism and individualist reformation a two level conflict can be observed. One issue, the power of Rome and papal obedience facing personal conviction reformers and in counterpoint the theme of political freedom, as it moved between monarchic command and rebellion. The two matters were not resolved, command passing from Catholic King opposed to protestants, then Protestant King passing law of tolerance, only then to cross over to Rome. "Paris is worth a Mass!" The won freedom of religion – which lasted only a century was the result of monarchy becoming absolute. Thus the gain of religious freedom emerged as state power became absolute.

The revocation of the Edict of Nantes in 1685 puts the last act of absolutism in place and certainly paved the way for its last phase.

With Henri IV granting freedom of religion at exactly the same time as he assumes the national throne as an absolute monarch blurred the impact of absolutism. Yet it is after Henry in turn was murdered, leaving a Bourbon absolutism in place, that the true matter of political freedom in its Roman sense could emerge.

4

LA FRONDE

I t is only in the Bourbon years that the high affair of free consultation at the top, the Brutus subject, was able to express itself and at least practice its business in open discourse. It involved firstly the judges, then the parliament, then the high aristocracy.

From 1648–1652 France tasted liberty in the Roman manner. It was Louis XIV's legal maturity that ended it, plunging France into a darkness from which it has never recovered, choosing as it has continued to do, the Augustan compromise – the name of Republic and the reality of absolutism.

This high passage in European history, embodying France's greatest epoch is called, ironically, La Fronde.

What is seemed to be – a sling aimed at a powerful target – and what it was in political theory were two very different things.

Voltaire the morally dubious father of both Jacobin terror and Napoleonic 'gloire' dismisses "La Fronde – commedia buffa!" Entombed in the atheist temple of revolutionary heroes, the Pantheon, he bore witness to the light of reason but could not confront the Marquis de Sade's dark psychic identity, ironically the most important of the few prisoners still in the Bastille when it was 'liberated.' Voltaire, a republican who lived off princes, had a very narrow view of the human creature. La Fronde takes its place both in the central stream of French history and that of a rich, complex humanity never to be met with again – Cardinal de Retz, Madame de Sévigné, les Condé, la Rochefoucauld, Corneille.

Simone Weil in her 'The Need for Roots' wrote: 'During the Fronde and under Mazarin, France, in spite of the general distress was morally able to breathe,' something that she knew had never happened again up to the modern epoch culminating as it did with a German occupation followed by an American conquest.

Put simply, the state educated French student does not know his own history. If the Revolution is set as the pivotal event of national identity it means to re-construct everything prior to it as primitive, unjust and hierarchical. The famed egalité certainly abolished titles, but its fiduciary aspect was carefully hidden. Vast wealth is the product of the Republic and the Napoleonic phases of rule. Monarchy is set up as 'ancien régime', elected government is the new. But the post-Roman history of France is just not that simple, indeed, very little is known about it. There is the sketchilly outlined epoch of barbarian mass influx from the east, there is the gradual collapse of Roman rule, i.e. taxation and the equally gradual emergence of local castle-based governance and protection followed by the slow emergence of 'les grands', the ruling of France in discrete zones, Armagnac, Burgundy, Normandie and so on, then Merovingian kingship yielding to the hereditary line of the Capetians, just prior to 1000. Even then the monarchy remained elective for 200 years, only becoming legally inherited with Philippe II Auguste. From 1300 under the rule of Philippe IV Le Bel up until 1600 monarchy itself evolved and became powerful yet at the same time the inner fabric of France became webbed with civic patterns of justice, taxation and local governance.

With the ghastly power of Rome's universalism challenged both by scholars and finally, rulers, within its still working system the doctrine of the state began to emerge as narrated in Laski's magisterial analysis.

The emergent absolutism of the Bourbons firmly in place, the price, quite literally, began to be felt by the common people.

La Fronde was, in effect, the French Revolution. It failed. What resulted once the Bourbons degenerated was, in 1797, the bloodbath. It was not the beginning it was the end. To the French at the time, La Fronde was seen as a storm, a tempest, a whirlwind. To the more politically sophisticated Italians there was no doubt. The Venetian, Count Gualdo Priorato in 1655 published his study, "History of the Revolution in France." However, now that we can re-appraise the French Revolution of 1789 as the site of the complete disintegration of an ancient and functioning state system, similar in violence and total re-evaluation of civic rules to what happened in Russia in 1917, it is more correct to grant the term to both 1797 and 1917. This permits us to say that America in 1776 had a coup d'état followed by de-colonisation and that France from 1648-52 attempted to recover consultative government, limit monarchic power, eliminate unjust taxes and restore legality to the state's judgments and rule back to entities free of Catholic and monarchic compulsion.

La Fronde brought together the Judges, the Parliament and the great families, something never before achieved and never repeated after. Together they fought to curb taxation, to remove value-added tax on consumer goods, and crippling excises on the internal movement of goods.

In the bankrupt – to America – condition of Europe after World War II a small value-added tax on all goods was imposed on an exhausted and unprotesting public.

Over the years it has annually increased. It is presented as a natural phenomenon, part of life, unquestioned. Yet it remains the vital principle both physical and psychological which now controls world finance.

La Fronde seems to be not just the first but the only attempt to dismantle the foundation of capitalism, money-supply-one, the indirect taxation on all sales then ironically named 'les aides.'

It also attacked the continual practice of building into a 'rente' or a contract an increase in the exchange, that is, the usurious principle denounced then by the Catholic Church but used daily by the absolute monarchic system.

Henry IV's absolute rule submitted all lands to the throne. Presented as an abolition of fiefdom, thus an evolutionary step away from old feudalism, it was, of course, the dissolution of local government. 1607 marked the end of the fiefs and with it went the aristocratic role of local protector.

The final phase of La Fronde, now named the Prince's Fronde as if it was separate rather than a culmination uniting all society, marked by its failure the end of the protecting aristocracy, friend of the people.

The collapse of La Fronde was the beginning of the adult rule of Louis XIV. On ascending the national throne he began a long reign in which he shunned Paris, the seat of the abandoned Parliament. He settled in Versailles which he transformed into a vast factory the function of which was to turn the aristocracy from warriors into courtiers. The dismal descent from brave military leader to abject man of the court can be traced in one family, the great Condé branch of the Bourbons so feared for their leadership at the end of La Fronde.

When, years later, Napoleon had ignominiously had the Duc d'Enghien executed, he did not do so to cut the Bourbon royal line. He was politically much more astute. He ended that awakening of La Fronde which Condé symbolised – the very thing his absolutism feared.

Once we have understood that the Roman Republic did not fail – it was a model which was rejected, it becomes possible to see that La Fronde did not fail – it was a model which was rejected.

In 1651 the rule of Louis XIV's majority, Mazarin was left in place. Although the implacable enemy of La Fronde he was shaped and indeed survived on its twists and turns. Thus his last decade still echoes with the memory of freedom. The coming of Colbert, the proto-banker, marks the beginning of the end. In 1661 the personal rule of the dictator begins, climaxing with the Revocation of the Edict of Nantes and with Protestantism again outside the law. The Catholic Church was not torn away from the state until 1904!

When we measure La Fronde as the last chance of Roman republicanism, that is a governance in limited power over a limited period and sustaining political colloquy without the co-ercion of physical restraint and fear, it becomes clear that the collapse of the state was both rapid and disastrous. Once the stages of dictatorship, seen as stasis, are removed, the decline and fall of France are markedly sudden and inevitable. Three dictatorships interrupt the tragedy.

Post-Roman France in End-Game

Three phases of dictatorial stasis.

1651 – 1715 Louis XIV.

1804 – 1815 Napoleon I.

1852 – 1870 Napoleon III.

The French Revolution is an event not with one but several historical narratives. On its 200th anniversary its celebrations were paid for by the banks. The legend is most appropriately encased in the narrative of a great poet. Lamartine's "Histoire des Girondins" despite, or because of its invented world is more significant that the more sober accounts written under a historian's discipline by Taine and Michelet. Mona Ozouf, who with Francois Furet, helped de-mythologise the revolutionary period, wrote an important and disturbing analysis of the Lamartine text on its re-edition. It is clear from her introduction that the wild and contradictory world of the Revolution has been re-instituted in modern minds and the Lamartine opus in fact has become the ur-version of the legend which replaces the historical critique – of whatever view – with a determinist recounting that both hides its contradictions and failures with a model which justifies everything, yes everything that came after.

Look at what followed the overthrow of the exhausted monarchism, a society theist having denied religion, rationalist and plunged into mass slaughter by drowning, sword, lamp-post and guillotine, a ruthless misogynism, and the creation of a monistic state defined as one and indivisible, which had precisely been the claim of absolute monarchy. It changed the legal Lèse majesté to Lèse nation!

The disaster unfolded rapidly. In exactly the same time it took the American settlers in tents to sweep across a continent, ship in thousands of African slaves then set them loose, slaughter then herd into a few village concentration camps the original nations of the continent – Sioux, Navaho, Algonquin, Apache, all forgotten as the new nation embarked on Empire, first in Asia and finally after conquering Europe, ending up in Arabia and Afghanistan – in exactly that same brief period, France collapsed.

After the Revolution and its first so-called Republic in 1792 came military dictatorship, as Ferguson had expected.

1804. Napoleon and Empire.

1815. Waterloo

1815 – 1848. Sub-Bourbon kings.

1848 – 1870. Napoleon III and Empire.

1848. Revolution and 2nd Republic.

1870. as named by Zola 'Débacle,' saw the siege of Paris and German occupation.

On the next year the bloodbath of La Commune in 1871, then 3rd Republic.

Gustave Flaubert wrote: 'Les bêtises de la republique depassent celles de l'empire.' 11 October 1871.

1914 – 19. World War One declared and controlled by the new political class commanding the mass slaughter from Paris. This marks the irrecoverable un-manning of a generation, that is de-generacy.

1939. World War Two declared and controlled by a government basically without an army.

1940. Armistice with Germany and second occupation.

1941. France divided by Germany into two zones.

1943. Total occupation of France by Germany.

1944. America invades France.

1946. Fifth Republic of de Gaulle.

1954 – 62. Algerian war of Independence.

1968. De Gaulle sells France's dollars and buys gold. His recognition that power is in the dollar currency system, secunding all political programme, and thus the Republic itself, leads to his de-mission and effectively the abolition of the Republican State now replaced by fiduciary, global transactions.

In historical terms, from 1792 – 1968 is a tsunami.

5

MARLOWE AND 'THE MASSACRE AT PARIS'

Laski's insight triumphs over his experience, Marlowe's knowledge triumphs over his.

Marlowe's direct experience of the egotism of power and the deceptions of the state resulted in the illumination of his work and the darkness of his death.

The nineteenth century raised up Marlowe as precursor and prologue to Shakespeare. His importance was seen in his forging of the iambic pentameter, what Ben Jonson called 'Marlowe's mighty line.' The twentieth century invented but could not sustain the fantasy of Marlowe as the first defender of a third sex identity. Modern homosexuality as defined by its authors, Foucault etc., simply did not exist in the Renaissance, and in any case, is not the theme of 'Edward II'. Marlowe's version of Ovid's Elegies and his long poem, Hero and Leander, called by Cheney a 'sublime portraiture of young love', mark him as a supreme upholder of love between men and women.

Marlowe as classicist, poet and dramatist is in all his work unceasingly forced to confront the nature of political power and its source in the individual whether pursuing a personal concern or a social ambition.

The twenty-first century saw the maturing of the Marlovian image. While some American scholars clung obsessively to a view which found sodomy in every metaphor, the train of thought had at last pulled into the republican station. It is now possible to see Marlowe as one of a trio of post-monarchist intellectuals, each in his own way re-evaluating the power nexus and acting beyond its then given order. Marlowe, Ralegh and Essex, each one murdered by the state yet already each thinking within a set of principles that are both Tacitean and post-christian. Recognising them as linked together it is also possible to see more clearly the two opposing positions on power. On the one hand the structuralist group view of the Cecils and the treacherous scientism of Bacon and on the other hand the elitist chivalric view, the former a humanism leading to dictatorship and the latter an individualism leading to an over-reaching of the self.

Essex in deconstructing his role as cavaliere servente, as a classicist came to see that society was dependent for its social health not on a leader but a bonded group of noblemen with honour. During his military campaigns he conferred 28 knighthoods in Normandy, 9 knighthoods on the Azores voyage, 24 knighthoods in Rouen and 81 knighthoods in Ireland. Essex was reconstructing the state. Elizabeth knew the issue had gone way beyond her personal neurotic obsession. Her god-son, Sir John Harrington wrote of her crying out, 'I am no Queen! That man is above me!' Essex's life now in imminent danger, he declared to the Lord Keeper: 'What, cannot princes err? Is an earthly power or authority infinite?' Essex had formulated the central thesis of the 'Vindiciae Contra Tyrannos.'

The poet Edmund Spenser named Essex as 'Great England's glory and the World's wide wonder.' Earl Marshal of England and

Chancellor of Cambridge University, Essex moved among the elite circles of the military and the academic. A confirmed Tacitean he made constant reference to him in his political analyses.

Sir Walter Ralegh, too, was a known Tacitean. In court circles the ambitions of Ralegh and Essex portrayed them as deadly enemies, but contemporary historians project their own bourgeois evaluation on two aristocrats both politically and intellectually in harmony. Paul Hyland in his moving 'Ralegh's Last Journey' recounts the scene of Ralegh's bearing on the scaffold.

"His notes reminded him to deal with one much older grievance and he said he would borrow a little more of Mr Sherrif's time to speak of an imputation that made his heart bleed: that he was a persecutor of Essex, that he stood in a window and puffed out smoke in disdain when he suffered. Stuckley accused him of repeating that Essex 'died like a fool, and like a coward, so persecuting his ghost and insolently trampling in his ashes.' Ralegh now said that he wept when Essex died.

'I confess indeed I was of a contrary faction, but I knew my Lord of Essex was a noble gentleman … and my soul hath been many times grieved that I was not nearer with him when he died, because I understood that he asked for me at his death, to be reconciled unto me.'

In a moment he would render up his account to God and, he protested, what he had spoken was true and he hoped he would be believed."

In the 'England's Helicon' published in 1650 Sir Walter Ralegh responded to Marlowe's 'The Passionate Shepherd to his Love' with a tributary poem entitled, 'The Nymph's Reply'. Richard Cholmeley, a spy of the Cecils, who moved in the Earl of Essex circle, declared that Marlowe was 'able to show more sound reasons for atheism than any divine in England is able to prove divinity, and that Marlowe told him, he hath read the atheist lecture to Sir Walter Ralegh and others.'

In Elizabethan usage atheism did not entail denial of god but rather abandonment of Christianity. Here were three intellectuals who had moved on, Tacitean, and republican by taste, openly disillusioned by absolutism in state and religion. Elizabeth was to execute Essex at mortal cost to herself and finality to Tudor rule. Marlowe was assassinated with her passive if not active connivance. Ralegh was to be executed by her heir, James I. Trevelyan said, 'the ghost of Ralegh pursued the House of Stuart to the scaffold.'

Marlowe was a classicist who became a playwright. His poetry contains the highest aspect of his genius. His rendering of Ovid's Elegies brought to the Elizabethan public a Roman poet who, exiled by Augustus, saw in poetry an exaltation of his freedom from monarchism. His version of Lucan's First Book of the Pharsalia is important because of its articulation of the view that in the Caesarean, that is, dictator's impulse to dominance is embedded a profound psychosis, a compulsive hurtling to disaster. Lucan points it out in Caesar, in Alexander, and by necessity in Emperor Nero. This madness lies opposite to the reasonableness of Cicero, of Cato, and of course his uncle, Seneca. A sign of his advanced thinking on power and rulership can be found in the question he asked when accused of counterfeiting 'French Crownes pistoletes and English shillinges'. He asked, 'did he not have as good Right to Coine as the Queen of England?' In locating power in the minting of coin he raised an issue that is still unanswered today hundreds of years later.

In Marlowe we are dealing with a more complex and participant intellect than that of his famous contemporaries. Native genius as a poet combined with his classical erudition had produced a unique personality clearly at home among the Tacitean elite and not belonging to the obedient world of playwrights.

There is a general consensus among critics today that while the text of 'The Massacre at Paris' is a late record of the play, truncated and incomplete, nevertheless it stands as Marlowe's final play.

In the mixed bag of the Cambridge Companion to Marlowe, Sara Munson Deats writes:

'No one, to my knowledge, questions Marlowe as the sole author of the work, and critical presumption, based primarily on Henslowe's Diary, agrees on 1592 as the probable date of the play's composition and 26 January 1593 as the drama's stage debut. Henslowe also identifies The Massacre as an early modern blockbuster, the highest grossing play of the season for Lord Strange's Men.'

Defining the surviving text as a 'pirated memorial reconstruction' she concludes:

'Moreover, in a historical period wracked with religious terrorism The Massacre, with its brutal depiction of sectarian violence and realpolitik manoeuvring, seems painfully contemporary.'

Also in the Cambridge Companion, Paul Whitfield White, writes:

'Certainly, even as it stands, the surviving text shows religiously motivated violence on both sides and raises questions posed in the Tamburlaine plays and 'The Jew of Malta' about the cynical exploitation of religious authority and religiously induced fear in the pursuit of military force and political power.'

And in the same compilation David Riggs makes an important political point:

> 'The Massacre reveals that Marlowe had an intricate, firsthand knowledge of the French Civil Wars. It includes details that were not available from printed sources, and this bears out the hypothesis that he had performed diplomatic or secret-service work in France.... Queen Elizabeth paid the fatal compliment of taking him seriously, as a political agent to be reckoned with.'

Park Honan writes:

> 'For help, he was to draw amply on the vast publications mountain, especially on a study by the Huguenot lawyer Françoise Hotman, translated into English in 1573 as 'A true and plaine report of the Furious Outrages of Fraunce'. Among other works, he used Jean de Serres's bulky history, 'Civil Warres of France' (1574) and Simon Goulart's 'Memoires de l'Etat de France sous Charles Neuviēme' (1576); and he drew on spoken accounts and a balance of pro-Catholic and Huguenot pamphlets.
> ('Christopher Marlowe, Poet and Spy' Oxford 2005)

David Riggs, in his own study, quite the best contemporary work on Marlowe, sees his author as an insider on the political scene.

'When he reached the mid-1580s, however, Marlowe became a source in his own right. He had an intimate firsthand knowledge of the feud between King Henry III and the Guise. Much of the factual material in the latter part of The Massacre can only be verified by recourse to confidential sources in the State Papers. Marlowe obtained this information by word of mouth, from men who had been witness to these events. In contrast to the partisan account of Protestant and Catholic pamphleteers, he gives an even-handed, densely factual report on the feud. The brief documentary scenes that succeed one another in The Massacre at Paris resemble diplomatic dispatches: these were the raw materials of intelligence fieldwork.'

> Riggs sums up:
> 'To judge simply from what the actors remembered, Marlowe was evolving away from the stage and towards a more direct confrontation with the history of his own times.'
> 'The World of Christopher Marlowe' (Fraser 2004)

THE MASSACRE
AT PARIS

Christopher Marlowe

Scene I

Enter CHARLES *the French King,* [CATHERINE] *the* QUEEN-MOTHER, *the* KING OF NAVARRE, *the* PRINCE OF CONDÉ, *the* LORD HIGH ADMIRAL, *and* [MARGARET] *the* QUEEN OF NAVARRE, *with others.*

CHARLES

    Prince of Navarre my honourable brother,
    Prince Condé, and my good Lord Admiral,
    I wish this union and religious league,
    Knit in these hands, thus joined in nuptial rites,
    May not dissolve, till death dissolve our lives,
    And that the native sparks of princely love,
    That kindled first this motion in our hearts,
    May still be fuelled in our progeny.

NAVARRE

    The many favours which your grace hath shown,
    From time to time, but specially in this,
    Shall bind me ever to your highness' will,
    In what queen-mother or your grace commands.

CATHERINE
    Thanks, son Navarre, you see we love you well
    That link you in marriage with our daughter here;
    And, as you know, our difference in religion
    Might be a means to cross you in your love.

CHARLES
    Well Madam, let that rest.
    And now, my lords, the marriage-rites performed,
    We think it good to go and consummate
    The rest with hearing of a holy mass.
    Sister, I think yourself will bear us company.

MARGARET
    I will my good Lord.

CHARLES
    The rest that will not go, my lords, may stay
    Come, mother, let us go to honour this solemnity.

CATHERINE [*aside*]
    Which I'll dissolve with blood and cruelty.
    Exeunt the KING [CHARLES], *the* QUEEN-MOTHER, *and*
    the QUEEN OF NAVARRE [*with others*]; NAVARRE,
    the PRINCE OF CONDÉ, *and the* LORD HIGH ADMIRAL
    remain.

NAVARRE
    Prince Condé, and my good Lord Admiral,
    Now Guise may storm, but do us little hurt,
    Having the king, queen-mother on our sides,
    To stop the malice of his envious heart

That seeks to murder all the protestants.
Have you not heard of late how he decreed
If that the King had given consent thereto,
That all the protestants that are in Paris
Should have been murdered the other night?

ADMIRAL

My lord, I marvel that th'aspiring Guise
Adventure dares without the king's consent,
To meddle or attempt such dangerous things.

CONDÉ

My lord, you need not marvel at the Guise,
For what he doth the Pope will ratify,
In murder, mischief, or in tyranny.

NAVARRE

But He that sits and rules above the clouds
Doth hear and see the prayers of the just,
And will revenge the blood of innocents
That Guise hath slain by treason of his heart,
And brought by murder to their timeless ends.

ADMIRAL

My lord, but did you mark the Cardinal,
The Guise's brother, and the Duke Dumaine,
How they did storm at these your nuptial rites,
Because the house of Bourbon now comes in
And joins your lineage to the crown of France?

NAVARRE

And that's the cause that Guise so frowns at us

And beats his brains to catch us in his trap,
Which he hath pitched within his deadly toil.
Come, my lords, let's go to Church and pray
That God may still defend the right of France
And make His Gospel flourish in this land.

Exeunt.

SCENE II

Enter the DUKE OF GUISE.

GUISE

    If ever Hymen loured at marriage-rites,

    And had his altars decks with dusky lights;

    If ever sun stained heaven with bloody clouds,

    And made it look with terror on the world;

    If ever day were turned to ugly night,

    And night made semblance of the hue of hell;

    This day, this hour, this fatal night,

    Shall fully show the fury of them all.

    Apothecary!

               Enter the APOTHECARY.

APOTHECARY

    My lord?

GUISE

    Now shall I prove and guerdon to the full,

    The love thou bear'st unto the house of Guise.

    Where are those perfumed gloves which I sent

    To be poisoned? Hast thou done them? Speak!

    Will every savour breed a pang of death?

APOTHECARY

See where they be, my good lord,

And he that smells but to them dies.

GUISE

Then thou remainest resolute?

APOTHECARY

I am, my lord, in what your grace commands,

Till death.

GUISE

Thanks, my good friend, I will requite thy love.

Go, then, present them to the Queen Navarre;

For she is that huge blemish in our eye,

That makes these upstart heresies in France:

Be gone my friend, present them to her straight.

Exit APOTHECARY.

Soldier!

Enter a SOLDIER.

SOLDIER

My lord?

GUISE

Now come thou forth and play thy tragic part.

Stand in some window opening near the street,

And when thou see'st the Admiral ride by,

Discharge thy musket and perform his death,

And then I'll guerdon thee with store of crowns.

SOLDIER

    I will, my lord.
                    Exit.

GUISE

    Now, Guise, begin those deep-engendered thoughts
    To burst abroad those never-dying flames
    Which cannot be extinguished but by blood.
    Oft have I levelled, and at last have learned
    That peril is the chiefest way to happiness,
    And resolution honour's fairest aim.
    What glory is there in a common good
    That hangs for every peasant to achieve?
    That like I best that flies beyond my reach.
    Set me to scale the high pyramids,
    And thereon set the diadem of France;
    I'll either rend it with my nails to naught,
    Or mount the top with my aspiring wings,
    Although my downfall be the deepest hell.
    For this I wake, when others think I sleep,
    For this I wait, that scorns attendance else,
    For this, my quenchless thirst whereon I build,
    Hath often pleaded kindred to the king.
    For this, this head, this heart, this hand and sword,
    Contrives, imagines and fully executes
    Matters of import aimed at by many,
    Yet understood by none.
    For this, hath heaven engendered me of earth,
    For this, this earth sustains my body's weight,
    And with this wait I'll counterpoise a crown,
    Or with seditions weary all the world.

For this, from Spain the stately Catholics
Send Indian gold to coin me French *écues*;
For this have I a largess from the Pope,
A pension and a dispensation too;
And by that privilege to work upon,
My policy hath framed religion.
Religion: *O Diabole!*
Fie, I am ashamed, how ever that I seem,
To think a word of such a simple sound,
Of so great matter should be made the ground.
The gentle king, whose pleasure uncontrolled
Weak'neth his body and will waste his realm,
If I repair not what he ruinates –
Him, as a child, I daily win with words,
So that for proof he barely bears the name;
I execute, and he sustains the blame.
The mother queen works wonders for my sake,
And in my love entombs the hope of France,
Rifling the bowels of her treasury,
To supply my wants and necessity.
Paris hath full five hundred colleges –
As monasteries, priories, abbeys and halls –
Wherein are thirty thousand able men,
Besides a thousand sturdy student Catholics;
And more – of my knowledge, in one cloister keeps
Five hundred fat Franciscan friars and priests.
All this, and more, if more may be comprised,
To bring the will of our desires to end.
Then, Guise, since thou hast all the cards within thy hands
To shuffle or cut, take this as surest thing:
That, right or wrong, thou deal thyself a king.

Ay, but Navarre, Navarre, 'tis but a nook of France.
Sufficient yet for such a petty king,
That, with a rabblement of his heretics,
Blinds Europe's eyes and troubleth our estate:
Him will we –

Pointing to his sword.

But first let's follow those in France
That hinder our possession to the crown.
As Caesar to his soldiers, so say I:
Those that hate me will I learn to loath.
Give me a look that, when I bend the brows,
Pale death may walk in furrows of my face,
A hand that with a grasp may grip the world,
An ear to hear what my detractors say,
A royal seat, a sceptre, and a crown;
That those which do behold, they may become
As men that stand and gaze against the sun.
The plot is laid, and things shall come to pass,
Where resolution strives for victory.

Exit.

Scene III

Enter the KING OF NAVARRE *and* QUEEN [MARGARET], *and his* MOTHER QUEEN [*the* OLD QUEEN], *the* PRINCE OF CONDÉ, *the* ADMIRAL, *and the* APOTHECARY *with the gloves, and he gives them to the* OLD QUEEN.

APOTHECARY

Ma'am, I beseech your grace accept this simple gift.

OLD QUEEN

Thanks, my good friend. Hold, take thou this reward.

APOTHECARY.

I humbly thank your majesty.
> *Exit* APOTHECARY.

OLD QUEEN

Methinks the gloves have a very strong perfume,
The scent whereof doth make my head to ache.

NAVARRE

Doth not your grace know the man that gave them you?

OLD QUEEN
    Not well, but do remember such a man.

ADMIRAL
    Your grace was ill-advised to take them, then,
    Considering of these dangerous times.

OLD QUEEN
    Help, son Navarre, I am poisoned!

MARGARET
    The heavens forbid your highness such mishap!

NAVARRE
    The late suspicion of the duke of Guise
    Might well have moved your highness to beware
    How you did meddle with such dangerous gifts.

MARGARET
    Too late it is, my lord, if that be true,
    To blame her highness, but I hope it be
    Only some natural passion makes her sick.

OLD QUEEN.
    O, no, sweet Margaret, the fatal poison
    Works within my head; my brain-pan breaks,
    My heart doth faint, I die!
              She dies.

NAVARRE
    My mother poisoned here before my face!
    O gracious God, what times are these?

O grant, sweet God, my days may end with hers,
That I with her may die and live again.

MARGARET

Let not this heavy chance, my dearest lord,
For whose effects my soul is massacred,
Infect thy gracious breast with fresh supply,
To aggravate our sudden misery.

ADMIRAL

Come, my lords, let us bear her body hence,
And see it honoured with solemnity.
            As they are going, the SOLDIER *dischargeth*
            his musket at the LORD ADMIRAL.

CONDÉ

What, are you hurt, my lord High Admiral?

ADMIRAL

Ay, my good lord, shot through the arm.

NAVARRE

We are betrayed! Come, my lords, and let us go tell
the King of this.

ADMIRAL

These are the cursed Guisians that do seek our death.
O, fatal was this marriage to us all.
            They bear away the [OLD] QUEEN *and go out.*

Scene IV

Enter the KING [CHARLES], [CATHERINE *the*] QUEEN-MOTHER, *the* DUKE OF GUISE, DUKE ANJOU, DUKE DEMAINE, [COSSIN *and* ATTENDANTS].

CATHERINE
    My noble son, and princely duke of Guise,
    Now have we got the fatal straggling deer
    Within the compass of a deadly toil,
    And as we late decreed we may perform.

CHARLES
    Madam, it will be noted through the world
    An action bloody and tyrannical –
    Chiefly since under safety of our word
    They justly challenge their protection.
    Besides, my heart relents that noble men,
    Only corrupted in religion,
    Ladies of honour, knights, and gentlemen,
    Should for their conscience taste such ruthless ends.

ANJOU
    Though gentle minds should pity others' pains,

Yet will the wisest note their proper griefs,
And rather seek to scourge their enemies
Than be themselves base subjects to the whip.

GUISE

Methinks, my lord, Anjou hath well advised
Your highness to consider of the thing,
And rather choose to seek your country's good,
Than pity or relieve these upstart heretics.

CATHERINE

I hope these reasons may serve my princely son
To have some care for fear of enemies.

CHARLES

Well, madam, I refer it to your majesty,
And to my nephew here, the duke of Guise:
What you determine, I will ratify.

CATHERINE

Thanks to my princely son. Then tell me, Guise,
What order will you set down for the massacre?

GUISE

Thus, madam:
They that shall be actors in this massacre
Shall wear white crosses on their burgonets,
And tie white linen scarfs about their arms;
He that wants these is suspect of heresy,
Shall die, be he king or emperor.
Then I'll have a peal of ordinance shot from the tower,
At which they all shall issue out and set the streets;

And then, the watchword being given, a bell shall ring,
Which when they hear, they shall begin to kill,
And never cease until that bell shall cease;
Then breathe a while.
                 Enter the ADMIRAL'S MAN.

CHARLES

How now, fellow, what news?

MAN

And it please your grace, the Lord High Admiral,
Riding the streets, was traitorously shot,
And most humble entreats your majesty
To visit him sick in his bed.

CHARLES

Messenger, tell him I will see him straight.
                 Exit [ADMIRAL'S MAN].
What shall we do now with the Admiral?

CATHERINE

Your majesty were best go visit him,
And make a show as if all were well.

CHARLES

Content, I will go visit the Admiral.

GUISE [*aside*]

And I will go take order for his death.
                 Exit.
                 Enter the ADMIRAL *in his bed.*

CHARLES

How fares it with my lord High Admiral,
Hath he been hurt with villains in the street?
I vow and swear, as I am King of France,
To find and to repay the man with death,
With death delayed and torments never used,
That durst presume, for hope of any gain,
To hurt the noble man their sovereign loves.

ADMIRAL

Ah, my good lord, these are the Guisians,
That seek to massacre our guiltless lives.

CHARLES

Assure yourself, my good Lord Admiral,
I deeply sorrow for your treacherous wrong,
And that I am not more secure myself,
Than I am careful you should be preserved.
Cossin, take twenty of our strongest guard,
And under your direction see they keep
All treacherous violence from our noble friend,
Repaying all attempts with present death,
Upon the cursed breakers of our peace.
And so be patient, good Lord Admiral,
And every hour I will visit you.

ADMIRAL

I humbly thank your royal majesty.

Exeunt.

Scene V

Enter GUISE, ANJOU, DUMAINE, GONZAGO, RETES,
MONTSORRELL, *and* SOLDIERS *to the massacre.*

GUISE

    Anjou, Dumaine, Gonzago, Retes, swear
    By the argent crosses in your burgonets
    To kill all that you suspect of heresy.

DUMAINE

    I swear by this to be unmerciful.

ANJOU

    I am disguised and none knows who I am,
    And therefore mean to murder all I meet.

GONZAGO

    And so will I.

RETES

    And I.

GUISE

    Away then, break into the Admiral's house.

RETES

    Ay, let the Admiral be first dispatched.

GUISE

    The Admiral,
    Chief standard-bearer to the Lutherans,
    Shall in the entrance of this massacre,
    Be murdered in his bed.
    Gonzago, conduct them thither, and then
    Beset his house, that not a man may live.

ANJOU

    That charge is mine. Switzers, keep you the streets;
    And at each corner shall the king's guard stand.

GONZAGO

    Come, sirs, follow me.
           Exit GONZAGO *and others with him.*

ANJOU

    Cossin, the captain of the Admiral's guard,
    Placed by my brother, will betray his lord.
    Now, Guise, shall Catholics flourish once again,
    The head being off, the members cannot stand.

RETES

    But look, my lord, there's some in the Admiral's house.
           Enter [GONZAGO *and others*] *into the* ADMIRAL'*s*
           house, and he in his bed.

ANJOU

In lucky time; come, let us keep this lane
And slay his servants that shall issue out.

GONZAGO

Where is the Admiral?

ADMIRAL

O, let me pray before I die!

GONZAGO

Then pray unto our Lady, kiss this cross.
Stab him.

ADMIRAL

O God, forgive my sins!
[*Dies.*]

GUISE

Gonzago, what, is he dead?

GONZAGO

Ay, my lord.

GUISE

Then throw him down.
[*The body of the ADMIRAL is thrown down.*]

ANJOU

Now, cousin, view him well;
It may be it is some other and he escaped.

GUISE

    Cousin, 'tis he, I know him by his look.

    See where my soldier shot him through the arm;

    He missed him near, but we have struck him now.

    Ah, base Shatillian and degenerate,

    Chief standard-bearer to the Lutherans,

    Thus in despite of thy religion,

    The duke of Guise stamps on thy lifeless bulk!

ANJOU

    Away with him! Cut off his head and hands,

    And send them for a present to the Pope;

    And when this just revenge is finished,

    Unto mount Faucon will we drag his corse,

    And he that living hated so the cross,

    Shall, being dead, be hanged thereon in chains.

GUISE

    Anjou, Gonzago, Retes, if that you three

    Will be as resolute as I and Dumaine,

    There shall not a Huguenot breathe in France.

ANJOU

    I swear by this cross, we'll not be partial,

    But slay as many as we can come near.

GUISE

    Mountsorrell, go shoot the ordnance off,

    That they which have already set the street

    May know their watchword, then toll the bell,

    And so let's forward to the massacre.

MOUNTSORRELL

    I will, my lord.

              Exit MOUNTSORRELL.

GUISE

    And now, my lords, let us closely to our business.

ANJOU

    Anjou will follow thee.

DUMAINE

    And so will Dumaine.

          The ordinance being shot off, the bell tolls.

GUISE

    Come, then, let's away.

                              Exeunt.

Scene VI

The GUISE *enters again, with all the rest, with their swords drawn, chasing the* PROTESTANTS.

GUISE
   Tue, tue, tue!
   Let none escape. Murder the Huguenots.

ANJOU
   Kill them, kill them!

                                                              Exeunt.

Scene VII

Enter LOREINE, *running; the* GUISE *and the rest pursuing him.*

GUISE

 Loreine, Loreine, follow Loreine! Sirrah,
 Are you a preacher of these heresies?

LOREINE

 I am a preacher of the word of God,
 And thou a traitor to thy soul and Him.

GUISE

 'Dearly beloved brother' – thus 'tis written.
    He stabs him [*and* LOREINE *dies*].

ANJOU

 Stay, my lord, let me begin the psalm.

GUISE

 Come, drag him away, and throw him in a ditch.

            Exeunt.

SCENE VIII

Enter MOUNTSORRELL *and knocks at* SEROUNE's *door.*

SEROUN'S WIFE [*within*]
  Who is that which knocks there?

MOUNTSORRELL
  Mountsorrell, from the duke of Guise.

SEROUN'S WIFE [*within*]
  Husband, come down, here's one would speak with
  you from the duke of Guise.
          Enter Seroune.

SEROUNE
  To speak with me, from such a man as he?

MOUNTSORRELL
  Ay, ay, for this, Seroune, and thou shalt ha't.
          Showing his dagger.

SEROUNE
  O, let me pray before I take my death.

MOUNTSORRELL

Dispatch then, quickly.

SEROUNE

O Christ, my saviour!

MOUNTSORRELL

Christ, villain? Why, dar'st thou presume to call on Christ,
Without the intercession of some saint?
Sanctus Jacobus, he was my saint; pray to him.

SEROUNE

O, let me pray unto my God.

MOUNTSORRELL.

Then take this with you.
Stab him. Exit.

Scene IX

Enter RAMUS *in his study.*

RAMUS
    What fearful cries come from the river Seine
    That frights poor Ramus sitting at his book?
    I fear the Guisians have passed the bridge,
    And mean once more to menace me.
             Enter TALEUS.

TALEUS
    Fly, Ramus, fly, if thou wilt save thy life.

RAMUS
    Tell me, Taleus, wherefore should I fly?

TALEUS
    The Guisians are hard at thy door,
    And mean to murder us.
    Hark, hark, they come. I'll leap out at the window.

RAMUS
    Sweet Taleus, stay.
             Enter GONZAGO *and* RETES.

GONZAGO

Who goes there?

RETES.

'Tis Taleus, Ramus' bedfellow.

GONZAGO

What art thou?

TALEUS

I am as Ramus is – a Christian.

RETES

O, let him go, he is a Catholic.
Exit TALEUS.

GONZAGO

Come Ramus, more gold, or thou shalt have the stab.

RAMUS

Alas, I am a scholar, how should I have gold?
All that I have is but my stipend from the king,
Which is no sooner received but it is spent.
                Enter the GUISE and ANJOU [*with* DUMAINE,
                MOUNTSORRELL, *and* SOLDIERS].

ANJOU

Who have you there?

RETES

'Tis Ramus, the king's Professor of Logic.

GUISE

Stab him.

RAMUS.

O, good my lord, wherein hath Ramus so offended?

GUISE

Marry, sir, in having a smack in all,
And yet didst never sound anything to the depth.
Was it not thou that scoff'dst the *Organon*,
And said it was a heap of vanities?
He that will be a flat dichotomist,
And seen in nothing but epitomes,
Is in your judgment thought a learned man;
And he, forsooth, must go and preach in Germany,
Excepting against doctors' axioms,
And *ipse dixi* with this quiddity,
Argumentum testimonii est inartificiale.
To contradict which, I say: Ramus shall die.
How answer you that? Your *nego argumentum*
Cannot serve, Sirrah. Kill him.

RAMUS

O, good my lord, let me but speak a word.

ANJOU. Well, say on.

RAMUS

Not for my life do I desire this pause,
But in my latter hour to purge myself,
In that I know the things that I have wrote,
Which, as I hear, one Sheckius takes it ill,

Because my places, being but three, contain all his.
I knew the *Organon* to be confused,
And I reduced it into better form;
And this for Aristotle will I say,
That he that despiseth him can ne'er
Be good in logic or philosophy;
And that's' because the blockish Sorbonnists
Attribute as much unto their works
As to the service of the eternal God.

GUISE

Why suffer you that peasant to declaim?
Stab him, I say, and send him to his friends in hell.

ANJOU.

Ne'er was there collier's son so full of pride.
Kills him.

GUISE

My lord Anjou, there are a hundred Protestants
Which we have chased into the river Seine
That swim about and so preserve their lives;
How may we do? I fear me they will live.

DUMAINE

Go place some men upon the bridge
With bows and darts to shoot at them they see,
And sink them in the river as they swim.

GUISE

'Tis well advised, Dumaine; go see it straight be done.
[*Exit* DUMAINE.]

And, in the meantime, my lord, could we devise
To get those pedants from the King Navarre
That are tutors to him and the prince of Condé —

ANJOU

For that, let me alone; cousin stay you here,
And when you see me in, then follow hard.

> He [ANJOU] *knocketh, and enter the* KING OF
> NAVARRE *and* [*the*] PRINCE OF CONDÉ, *with
> their* [*two*] SCHOOLMASTERS.

How now, my lords, how fare you?

NAVARRE

My lord, they say that all the Protestants are massacred.

ANJOU

Ay, so they are, but yet what remedy?
I have done what I could to stay this broil.

NAVARRE

But yet, my lord, the report doth run
That you were one that made this massacre.

ANJOU

Who, I? You are deceived, I rose but now.

> *Enter* [*to them*] GUISE [*with* GONZAGO, RETES,
> MOUNTSORRELL *and* SOLDIERS].

GUISE

Murder the Huguenots, take those pedants hence.

NAVARRE

    Thou traitor, Guise, lay off thy bloody hands.

CONDÉ

    Come, let us go tell the king.
            Exeunt [CONDÉ *and* NAVARRE].

GUISE

    Come sirs, I'll whip you to death with my poniard's point.
            He kills them [*the* SCHOOLMASTERS].

ANJOU

    Away with them both.
            Exit ANJOU [*with* SOLDIERS *carrying the bodies*].

GUISE

    And now, sirs, for this night let our fury stay.
    Yet will we not that the massacre shall end:
    Gonzago, post you to Orleans,
    Retes to Dieppe, Mountsorrell unto Rouen,
    And spare not one that you suspect of heresy.
    And now stay that bell, that to the devil's matins rings.
    Now every man put off his burgonet,
    And so convey him closely to his bed.

                                      Exeunt.

Scene X

Enter ANJOU, *with two* LORDS OF POLAND.

ANJOU

    My lords of Poland, I must needs confess
    The offer of your Prince Electors far
    Beyond the reach of my deserts;
    For Poland is, as I have been informed,
    A martial people, worthy such a king
    As hath sufficient counsel in himself
    To lighten doubts and frustrate subtle foes;
    And such a king whom practice long hath taught
    To please himself with manage of the wars,
    The greatest wars within our Christian bounds –
    I mean our wars against the Muscovites,
    And on the other side against the Turk,
    Rich princes both, and mighty emperors.
    Yet by my brother Charles, our king of France,
    And by his grace's council, it is thought
    That if I undertake to wear the crown
    Of Poland, it may prejudice their hope
    Of my inheritance to the crown of France;
    For, if th'almighty take my brother hence,

By due descent the regal seat is mine.
With Poland, therefore, must I covenant thus:
That if, by death of Charles, the diadem
Of France be cast on me, then with your leaves
I may retire me to my native home.
If your commission serve to warrant this,
I thankfully shall undertake the charge
Of you and yours, and carefully maintain
The wealth and safety of your kingdom's right.

FIRST LORD
All this and more your highness shall command
For Poland's crown and kingly diadem.

ANJOU
Then come, my lords, let's go.

Exeunt.

SCENE XI

Enter two [SOLDIERS] *with the* ADMIRAL'*s body.*

FIRST SOLDIER
    Now, sirrah, what shall we do with the Admiral?

SECOND SOLDIER
    Why, let us burn him for a heretic.

FIRST SOLDIER
    O no, his body will infect the fire, and the fire
    the air, and so we shall be poisoned with him.

SECOND SOLDIER
    What shall we do, then?

FIRST SOLDIER
    Let's throw him into the river.

SECOND SOLDIER
    O, 'twill corrupt the water, and the water
    the fish, and the fish ourselves when we eat them.

FIRST SOLDIER
    Then throw him into the ditch.

SECOND SOLDIER
    No, no, to decide all doubts, be ruled by me:
    let's hang him here upon this tree.

FIRST SOLDIER
    Agreed.
                    They hang him [*and exeunt*].
    Enter the DUKE OF GUISE, [CATHERINE *the*] QUEEN-
    MOTHER, *and the* CARDINAL [*with* ATTENDANTS].

GUISE
    Now, madam, how like you our lusty Admiral?

CATHERINE
    Believe me, Guise, he becomes the place so well
    As I could long ere this have wished him there.
    But come, let's walk aside, th'air's not very sweet.

GUISE
    No, by my faith, madam.
    Sirs, take him away and throw him in some ditch.
                    [*The* ATTENDANTS] *carry away the dead body.*
    And now, madam, as I understand,
    There are a hundred Huguenots and more
    Which in the woods do hold their synagogue,
    And daily meet about this time of day,
    And thither will I to put them to the sword.

CATHERINE

    Do so, sweet Guise, let us delay no time,

    For if these stragglers gather head again,

    And disperse themselves throughout the Realm of France,

    It will be hard for us to work their deaths.

    Be gone, delay no time, sweet Guise.

GUISE

    Madam, I go as whirlwinds rage before a storm.

             Exit.

CATHERINE

    My lord of Lorraine, have you marks of late

    How Charles, our son, begins for to lament

    For the late night's work which my lord of Guise

    Did make in Paris with the Huguenots?

CARDINAL

    Madam, I have heard him solemnly vow

    With the rebellious King of Navarre

    For to revenge their deaths upon us all.

CATHERINE

    Ay, but my lord, let me alone for that,

    For Catherine must have her will in France.

    As I do live, so surely shall he die,

    And Henry then shall wear the diadem;

    And if he grudge or cross his mother's will,

    I'll disinherit him and all the rest;

    For I'll rule France, but they shall wear the crown,

And, if they storm, I then may pull them down.
Come, my lord, let's go.

Exeunt.

SCENE XII

Enter five or six PROTESTANTS *with books, and kneel together.*
Enter also the GUISE *and* [*others*].

GUISE

    Down with the Huguenots! Murder them!

PROTESTANT

    O *monsieur de Guise*, hear me but speak!

GUISE

    No, villain, no that tongue of thine
    That hath blasphemed the holy Church of Rome,
    Shall drive no plaints into the Guise's ears
    To make the justice of my heart relent.
    Tue, tue, tue! Let none escape.
        Kill them.
    So, drag them away.

                            Exeunt.

Scene XIII

Enter the KING OF FRANCE, NAVARRE *and* EPERNOUN
staying him; enter [CATHERINE *the*] QUEEN-MOTHER, *and the*
CARDINAL [, PLESHÉ *and* ATTENDANTS].

CHARLES

    O, let me stay and rest me here a while,

    A griping pain hath seized upon my heart;

    A sudden pang, the messenger of death.

CATHERINE

    O say not so, thou kill'st thy mother's heart.

CHARLES

    I must say so; pain forceth me complain.

NAVARRE

    Comfort yourself, my lord, I have no doubt

    But God will sure restore you to your health.

CHARLES

    O no, my loving brother of Navarre!

    I have deserved a scourge, I must confess;

Yet is there patience of another sort
Than to misdo the welfare of their king:
God grant my nearest friends may prove no worse!
O hold me up, my sight begins to fail,
My sinews shrink, my brain turns upside down,
My heart doth break, I faint and die.

       He dies.

CATHERINE

What, art thou dead? Sweet son, speak to thy mother!
O no, his soul is fled from out his breast,
And he nor hears nor sees us what we do.
My lords, what resteth now for to be done,
But that we presently dispatch ambassadors
To Poland to call Henry back again
To wear his brother's crown and dignity.
Epernoun, go see it presently be done,
And bid him come without delay to us.

EPERNOUN

Madam, I will.

       Exit.

CATHERINE

And now, my lords, after these funerals be done,
We will, with all the speed we can, provide
For Henry's coronation from Polony.
Come, let us take his body hence.

       All go out but NAVARRE *and* PLESHÉ.

NAVARRE

    And now, Navarre, whilst that these broils do last,
    My opportunity may serve me fit
    To steal from France and hie me to my home,
    For here's no safety in the realm for me;
    And now that Henry is called from Poland,
    It is my due, by just succession;
    And therefore, as speedily as I can perform,
    I'll muster up an army secretly,
    For fear that Guise, joined with the King of Spain,
    Might seem to cross me in mine enterprise.
    But God that always doth defend the right
    Will show His mercy and preserve us still.

PLESHÉ

    The virtues of our true religion
    Cannot but march with many graces more,
    Whose army shall discomfort all your foes,
    And, at the length, in Pampelonia crown,
    (In spite of Spain and all the popish power
    That holds it from your highness wrongfully)
    Your majesty her rightful lord and sovereign.

NAVARRE

    Truth, Pleshé; and God so prosper me in all
    As I intend to labour for the truth
    And true profession of His holy word!
    Come, Pleshé, let's away while time doth serve.

Exeunt.

Scene XIV

Sound Trumpets within, and then all cry 'vive le roi' *two or three times. Enter* HENRY [ANJOU] *crowned;* [CATHERINE *the*] QUEEN [-MOTHER], CARDINAL, DUKE OF GUISE, EPERNOUN, *the King's Minions* [JOYEUX and MUGER-OUN], *with others, and the* CUTPURSE.

ALL
　Vive le roi, vive le roi!
　(*Sound Trumpets.*)

CATHERINE
　Welcome from Poland, Henry once again,
　Welcome to France, thy father's royal seat.
　Here hast thou a country void of fears,
　A warlike people to maintain thy right,
　A watchful senate for ordaining laws,
　A loving mother to preserve thy state,
　And all things that a king may wish besides;
　All this and more hath Henry with his crown.

CARDINAL
　And long may Henry enjoy all this, and more!

ALL

Vive le roi, vive le roi!

(*Sound Trumpets.*)

HENRY

Thanks to you all. The guider of all crowns
Grant that our deeds may well deserve your loves!
And so they shall, if fortune speed my will,
And yield your thoughts to height of my deserts.
What say our minions? Think they Henry's heart
Will not both harbour love and majesty?
Put off that fear, they are already joined.
No person, place, or time, or circumstance,
Shall slack my love's affection from his bent.
As now you are, so shall you still persist,
Removeless from the favours of your king.

MUGEROUN

We know that noble minds change not their thoughts
For wearing of a crown, in that your grace
Hath worn the Poland diadem before
You were invested in the crown of France.

HENRY

I tell thee, Mugeroun, we will be friends,
And fellows too, whatever storms arise.

MUGEROUN

Then may it please your majesty to give me leave
To punish those that do profane this holy feast.

He cuts off the CUTPURSE's *ear, for cutting of the gold buttons off his cloak.*

HENRY
How mean'st thou that?

CUTPURSE
O lord, mine ear!

MUGEROUN
Come, sir, give me my buttons and here's your ear.

GUISE [*to an* ATTENDANT]
Sirrah, take him away.

HENRY [*to* MUGEROUN]
Hands off, good fellow; I will be his bail
For this offence. [*To* CUTPURSE] Go, sirrah, work no more
Till this our coronation-day be past.
Our solemn rites of coronation done,
What now remains but for a while to feast
And spend some days in barriers, tourney, tilt,
And like disports, such as do fit the court?
Let's go, my lords, our dinner stays for us.
> *Go out all but the* [CATHERINE] *the* QUEEN
> [-MOTHER] *and the* CARDINAL.

CATHERINE
My lord Cardinal of Lorraine, tell me,
How likes your grace my son's pleasantness?
His mind, you see, runs on his minions,
And all his heaven is to delight himself;
And whilst he sleeps securely thus in ease,
Thy brother Guise and we may now provide
To plant ourselves with such authority

As not a man may live without our leaves.
Then shall the Catholic faith of Rome
Flourish in France, and none deny the same.

CARDINAL

Madam, as I in secrecy was told,
My brother Guise hath gathered a power of men,
Which are, he saith, to kill the Puritans;
But 'tis the house of Bourbon that he means.
Now, madam, must you insinuate with the king,
And tell him that 'tis for his country's good,
And common profit of religion.

CATHERINE

Tush, man, let me alone with him,
To work the way to bring this thing to pass;
And if he do deny what I do say,
I'll dispatch him with his brother presently.
And then shall monsieur wear the diadem,
Tush, all shall die unless I have my will,
For, while she lives, Catherine will be queen.
Come, my lord, let us go to seek the Guise,
And then determine of this enterprise.

Exeunt.

Scene XV

Enter the DUCHESS OF GUISE, *and her* MAID.

DUCHESS
Go fetch me pen and ink.
MAID. I will, madam.
Exit MAID.

DUCHESS
That I may write unto my dearest lord.
Sweet Mugeroun, 'tis he that hath my heart,
And Guise usurps it 'cause I am his wife.
Fain would I find some means to speak with him,
But cannot, and therefore am enforced to write
That he may come and meet me in some place
Where we may one enjoy the other's sight.
Enter the MAID *with* [*pen,*] *ink, and paper.*
So, set it down and leave me to myself.
Exit MAID.
She writes.
O would to God this quill that here doth write
Had late been plucked from out fair Cupid's wing,
That it might print these lines within his heart!

Enter the GUISE.

GUISE

    What, all alone, my love, and writing too?

    I prithee, say to whom thou writes?

DUCHESS

    To such a one, my lord, as when she reads my lines

    Will laugh, I fear me, at their good array.

GUISE

    I pray thee, let me see.

DUCHESS

    O no, my lord, a woman only must

    Partake the secrets of my heart.

GUISE

    But, madam, I must see.

            He takes it.

    Are these your secrets that no man must know?

DUCHESS

    O pardon me, my lord!

GUISE

    Thou trothless and unjust, what lines are these?

    Am I grown old, or is thy lust grown young,

    Or hath my love been so obscured in thee,

    That others needs to comment on my text?

    Is all my love forgot which held thee dear,

    Ay, dearer then the apple of mine eye?

Is Guise's glory but a cloudy mist,
In sight and judgement of thy lustful eye?
Mort dieu! Were't not the fruit within thy womb,
On whose increase I set some longing hope,
This wrathful hand should strike thee to the heart!
Hence, strumpet, hide thy head for shame,
And fly my presence, if thou look to live.
    Exit [DUCHESS].
O wicked sex, perjured and unjust,
Now do I see that from the very first
Her eyes and looks sowed seeds of perjury.
But, villain, he to whom these lines should go
Shall buy her love even with his dearest blood.

                Exit.

Scene XVI

Enter the KING OF NAVARRE, PLESHÉ *and* BARTUS, *and their train, with drums and trumpets.*

NAVARRE

    My lords, sith in a quarrel just and right
    We undertake to manage these our wars
    Against the proud disturbers of the faith,
    I mean the Guise, the Pope, and King of Spain,
    Who set themselves to tread us under foot,
    And rent our true religion from this land;
    But for you know our quarrel is no more
    But to defend their strange inventions,
    Which they will put us to with sword and fire;
    We must with resolute minds resolve to fight,
    In honour of our God and country's good.
    Spain is the council-chamber of the Pope,
    Spain is the place where he makes peace and war:
    And Guise for Spain hath now incensed the king
    To send his power to meet us in the field.

BARTUS

    Then in this bloody brunt they may behold

The sole endeavour of your princely care,
To plant the true succession of the faith
In spite of Spain and all his heresies.

NAVARRE

The power of vengeance now encamps itself
Upon the haughty mountains of my breast,
Plays with her gory colours of revenge,
Whom I respect as leaves of boasting green
That change their colour when the winter comes,
When I shall vaunt as victor in revenge.
Enter a MESSENGER.
How now, sirrah, what news?

MESSENGER

My lord, as by our scouts we understand,
A mighty army comes from France with speed,
Which is already mustered in the land,
And means to meet your highness in the field.

NAVARRE

In God's name, let them come!
This is the Guise that hath incensed the king
To levy arms and make these civil broils.
But canst thou tell me who is their general?

MESSENGER

Not yet, my lord, for thereon do they stay;
But, as report doth go, the duke of Joyeux
Hath made great suit unto the king therefore.

NAVARRE

    It will not countervail his pains, I hope
    I would the Guise in his stead might have come,
    But he doth lurk within his drowsy couch
    And makes his footstool on security;
    So he be safe, he cares not what becomes,
    Of king or country – no, not for them both.
    But come, my lords, let us away with speed
    And place ourselves in order for the fight.

Exeunt.

Scene XVII

Enter the KING OF FRANCE, DUKE OF GUISE, EPERNOUN, *and* DUKE JOYEUX.

HENRY
> My sweet Joyeux, I make thee general
> Of all my army, now in readiness
> To march against rebellious King Navarre.
> At thy request I am content thou go,
> Although my love to thee can hardly suffer't,
> Regarding still the danger of thy life.

JOYEUX
> Thanks to your majesty, and so I take my leave.
> Farwell my lord of Guise and Epernoun.

GUISE
> Health and hearty farewell to my lord Joyeux.
> > *Exit* JOYEUX.

HENRY
> So kindly, cousin of Guise, you and your wife
> Do both salute our lovely minions.

Remember you the letter, gentle sir,
Which your wife writ to my dear minion,
And her chosen friend?
> *He makes horns at the* GUISE.

GUISE

How now, my lord? Faith, this is more than need.
Am I thus to be jested at and scorned?
'Tis more than kingly or imperious;
And sure, if all the proudest kings in Christendom
Should bear me such derision, they should
Know how I scorned them and their mocks.
I love your minions? Dote on them yourself!
I know none else but holds them in disgrace.
And here by all the saints in heaven I swear,
That villain for whom I bear this deep disgrace –
Even for your words that have incensed me so –
Shall buy that strumpet's favour with his blood,
Whether he have dishonoured me or no!
Par la mort Dieu, il mourra!
> *Exit.*

HENRY

Believe me, this jest bites sore.

EPERNOUN

My lord, 'twere good to make them friends,
For his oaths are seldom spent in vain.
> *Enter* MUGEROUN.

HENRY

How now, Mugeroun? Met'st thou not the Guise at the door?

MUGEROUN

Not I, my lord; what if I had?

HENRY

Marry, if thou hadst, thou mightst have had the stab,
For he hath solemnly sworn thy death.

MUGEROUN

I may be stabbed, and live till he be dead.
But wherefore bears he me such deadly hate?

HENRY

Because his wife bears thee such kindly love.

MUGEROUN

If that be all, the next time that I meet her
I'll make her shake off love with her heels.
But which way is he gone? I'll go make a walk
On purpose from the court to meet with him.
Exit.

HENRY

I like not this. Come, Epernoun,
Let's go seek the duke and make them friends.

Exeunt.

Scene XVIII

Alarums, within. The DUKE JOYEUX *slain. Enter the* KING OF NAVARRE, *[with* BARTUS,*] and his train.*

NAVARRE

    The Duke is slain and all his power dispersed,

    And we are graced with wreathes of victory.

    Thus God, we see, doth ever guide the right

    To make his glory great upon the earth.

BARTUS

    The terror of this happy victory,

    I hope will make the king surcease his hate,

    And either never manage army more,

    Or else employ them in some better cause.

NAVARRE

    How many noble men have lost their lives

    In prosecution of these cruel arms,

    Is ruth and almost death to call to mind.

    But God, we know will always put them down

    That lift themselves against the perfect truth,

    Which I'll maintain as long as life doth last,

And with the Queen of England join my force
To beat the papal monarch from our lands,
And keep those relics from our countries' coasts.
Come, my lords, now that the storm is overpast,
Let us away with triumph to our tents.

Exeunt.

Scene XIX

Enter a SOLDIER [*with a musket*].

SOLDIER

    Sir, to you, sir, that dares make the duke a cuckold,
    and use a counterfeit key to his privy-chamber door; and
    although you take out nothing but your own, yet you put in
    that which displeaseth him, and so forestall his market and
    set up your standing where you should not; and whereas he
    is your landlord, you will take upon you to be his, and till the
    ground that he himself should occupy, which is his own free
    land – if it be not too free, there's the question. And though I
    come not to take possession (as I would I might), yet I mean
    to keep you out, which I will, if this gear hold. What, are ye
    come so soon? Have at ye, sir!

        Enter MUGEROUN. *He shoots at him and kills him.*
        Enter the GUISE [*and* ATTENDANTS].

GUISE

    Hold thee, tall soldier, take thee this and fly.

        Exit SOLDIER.

    Lie there, the king's delight and Guise's scorn.
    Revenge it, Henry, as thou list or dare,

I did it only in despite of thee.

              [ATTENDANTS] *take him away.*
            Enter the KING [HENRY] *and* EPERNOUN.

HENRY

    My lord of Guise, we understand that you
    Have gathered a power of men:
    What your intent is yet we cannot learn,
    But we presume it is not for our good.

GUISE

    Why, I am no traitor to the crown of France;
    What I have done, 'tis for the Gospel sake.

EPERNOUN

    Nay, for the Pope's sake, and thine own benefit.
    What peer in France but thou, aspiring Guise,
    Durst be in arms without the king's consent?
    I challenge thee for treason in the cause.

GUISE

    Ah, base Epernoun, were not his highness here,
    Thou shouldst perceive the duke of Guise is moved.

HENRY

    Be patient, Guise, and threat not Epernoun,
    Lest thou perceive the King of France be moved.

GUISE

    Why, I am a prince of the Valois' line,
    Therefore an enemy to the Bourbonites;
    I am a juror in the Holy League,

And therefore hated of the Protestants.
What should I do but stand upon my guard?
And, being able, I'll keep a host in pay.

EPERNOUN

Thou able to maintain a host in pay,
That livest by foreign exhibition!
The Pope and King of Spain are thy good friends,
Else all France knows how poor a Duke thou art.

HENRY

Ay, those are they that feed him with their gold,
To countermand our will and check our friends.

GUISE

My lord, to speak more plainly, thus it is:
Being animated by religious zeal,
I mean to muster all the power I can,
To overthrow those factious Puritans.
And know, my lord, the Pope will sell his triple crown,
Ay, and the catholic Philip, King of Spain,
Ere I shall want, will cause his Indians
To rip the golden bowels of America.
Navarre, that cloaks them underneath his wings,
Shall feel the house of Lorraine is his foe.
Your highness need not fear mine army's force;
'Tis for your safety and your enemies' wrack.

HENRY

Guise, wear our crown, and be thou King of France,
And as dictator make or war or peace,

Whilst I cry '*placet*' like a senator.
I cannot brook thy haughty insolence,
Dismiss thy camp, or else by our edict
Be thou proclaimed a traitor throughout France.

GUISE [*aside*]
  The choice is hard, I must dissemble.
    [*To* KING HENRY]
  My lord, in token of my true humility,
  And simple meaning to your majesty,
  I kiss your grace's hand and take my leave,
  Intending to dislodge my camp with speed.

HENRY
  Then farewell, Guise, the King and thou are friends.
    Exit GUISE.

EPERNOUN
  But trust him not, my lord, for had your highness
  Seen with what a pomp he entered Paris,
  And how the citizens with gifts and shows
  Did entertain him,
  And promised to be at his command –
  Nay, they feared not to speak in the streets
  That the Guise durst stand in arms against the king
  For not effecting of His Holiness' will.

HENRY
  Did they of Paris entertain him so?
  Then means he present treason to our state.
  Well, let me alone. Who's within there?

Enter one with a pen and ink.
Make a discharge of all my council straight,
And I'll subscribe my name and seal it straight.
My head shall be my council, they are false;
And, Epernoun, I will be ruled by thee.

EPERNOUN

My lord, I think for safety of your royal person,
It would be good the Guise were made away,
And so to quite your grace of all suspect.

HENRY

First let us set our hand and seal to this,
And then I'll tell thee what I mean to do.
            He writes.
So, convey this to the council presently;
            Exit one.
And Epernoun, though I seem mild and calm,
Think not but I am tragical within.
I'll secretly convey me unto Blois;
For, now that Paris takes the Guise's part,
Here is no staying for the King of France,
Unless he means to be betrayed and die.
But, as I live, so sure the Guise shall die.

                                        Exeunt.

Scene XX

Enter the KING OF NAVARRE, *reading of a letter, and* BARTUS.

NAVARRE

My lord, I am advertised from France
That the Guise hath taken arms against the king,
And that Paris is revolted from his grace.

BARTUS

Then hath your grace fit opportunity
To show your love unto the King of France,
Offering him aide against his enemies,
Which cannot but be thankfully received.

NAVARRE

Bartus, it shall be so; post then to France,
And there salute his highness in our name;
Assure him all the aid we can provide
Against the Guisians and their complices.
Bartus, be gone; commend me to his grace,
And tell him, ere it be long, I'll visit him.

BARTUS

I will, my lord.

Exit.

NAVARRE [*calling out*]
　Pleshé!

　　　　Enter PLESHÉ.

PLESHÉ
　My lord.

NAVARRE
　Pleshé, go muster up our men with speed,
　And let them march away to France amain,
　For we must aid the king against the Guise.
　Be gone, I say, 'tis time that we were there.

PLESHÉ
　I go, my lord.

　　　　　[*Exit* PLESHÉ.]

NAVARRE
　That wicked Guise, I fear me much, will be
　The ruin of that famous realm of France,
　For his aspiring thoughts aim at the crown,
　He takes his vantage on religion
　To plant the Pope and popelings in the realm,
　And bind it wholly to the Sea of Rome.
　But if that God do prosper mine attempts,
　And send us safely to arrive in France,
　We'll beat him back and drive him to his death
　That basely seeks the ruin of his realm.

　　　　　　　　　　　　　　　Exit.

Scene XXI

Enter the CAPTAIN OF THE GUARD, *and three* MURDERERS.

CAPTAIN
  Come on, sirs. what, are you resolutely bent,
  Hating the life and honour of the Guise?
  What, will you not fear, when you see him come?

FIRST MURDERER
  Fear him said you? Tush, were he here, we would kill him
  presently.

SECOND MURDERER
  O that his heart were leaping in my hand!

THIRD MURDERER
  But when will he come, that we may murder him?

CAPTAIN
  Well then, I see you are resolute.

FIRST MURDERER
  Let us alone, I warrant you.

CAPTAIN

Then, sirs, take your standings within this chamber,
For anon the Guise will come.

ALL

You will give us our money?

CAPTAIN

Ay, ay, fear not. Stand close, be resolute.
          [*The* MURDERERS *hide.*]
Now falls the star whose influence governs France,
Whose light was deadly to the Protestants.
Now must he fall and perish in his height.
                    Enter the KING [HENRY] *and* EPERNOUN.

HENRY

Now, captain of my guard, are these murderers ready?

CAPTAIN

They be, my good lord.

HENRY

But are they resolute and armed to kill,
Hating the life and honour of the Guise?

CAPTAIN

I warrant ye, my lord.

HENRY

Then come, proud Guise, and here disgorge thy breast
Surcharged with surfeit of ambitious thoughts;
Breathe out that life wherein my death was hid,

And end thy endless treasons with thy death.
Enter the GUISE *[within] and knocketh.*

GUISE

Holà, varlet, hé! [EPERNOUN *goes to the door*]
Epernoun, where is the King?

EPERNOUN

Mounted his royal cabinet.

GUISE

I prithee tell him that the Guise is here.

EPERNOUN

And please your grace, the duke of Guise, doth crave
Access unto your highness.

HENRY

Let him come in.
[*Aside*]
Come, Guise, and see thy traitorous guile outreached,
And perish in the pit thou mad'st for me.
The GUISE *comes to the* KING.

GUISE

Good morrow to your majesty.

HENRY

Good morrow to my loving cousin of Guise.
How fares it this morning with your excellence?

GUISE

    I heard your majesty was scarcely pleased

    That in the court I bear so great a train.

HENRY

    They were to blame that said I was displeased,

    And you, good cousin, to imagine it.

    'Twere hard with me if I should doubt my kin,

    Or be suspicious of my dearest friends.

    Cousin, assure you I am resolute –

    Whatsoever any whisper in mine ears –

    Not to suspect disloyalty in thee,

    And so, sweet coz, farewell.

                Exit KING [*with* EPERNOUN *and* CAPTAIN OF

                THE GUARD].

GUISE

    So, now sues the king for favour to the Guise,

    And all his minions stoop when I command.

    Why, this 'tis to have an army in the field.

    Now by the holy sacrament I swear,

    As ancient Romans o'er their captive lords,

    So will I triumph o'er this wanton king

    And he shall follow my proud chariot's wheels.

    Now do I but begin to look about,

    And all my former time was spent in vain.

    Hold, sword, for in thee is the duke of Guise's hope.

                Enter one of the MURDERERS.

    Villain, why dost thou look so ghastly? Speak!

THIRD MURDERER

O pardon me, my lord of Guise!

GUISE

Pardon thee? Why, what hast thou done?

THIRD MURDERER

O my lord, I am one of them that is set to murder you.

GUISE

To murder me, villain?

THIRD MURDERER

Ay, my lord; the rest have ta'en their standings in the next
room; therefore, good my lord, go not forth.

GUISE

Yet Caesar shall go forth.
Let mean conceits, and baser men fear death:
Tut, they are peasants, I am Duke of Guise;
And princes with their looks engender fear.
                    [*Enter two* MURDERERS]

FIRST MURDERER

Stand close, he is coming; I know him by his voice.

GUISE

As pale as ashes! Nay, then tis time to look about.

ALL

Down with him, down with him!
            They stab him.

GUISE

O, I have my death's wound! Give me leave to speak.

SECOND MURDERER

Then pray to God and ask forgiveness of the king.

GUISE

Trouble me not, I ne'er offended him,
Nor will I aske forgiveness of the king.
O, that I have not power to stay my life,
Nor immortality to be revenged!
To die by peasants, what a grief is this!
Ah, Sixtus, be revenged upon the king;
Philip and Parma, I am slain for you.
Pope, excommunicate, Philip, depose
The wicked branch of cursed Valois his line.
Vive la messe! Perish Huguenots!
Thus Caesar did go forth, and thus he dies.
        He dies.
        Enter CAPTAIN OF THE GUARD.

CAPTAIN

What, have you done? Then stay a while, and I'll go call the king.
But see where he comes.
        [*Enter the* KING, EPERNOUN
        and ATTENDANTS.]
My lord, see where the Guise is slain.

HENRY

Ah, this sweet sight is physic to my soul,

Go fetch his son for to behold his death.

[*Exit an* ATTENDANT.]

Surcharged with guilt of thousand massacres,
Monsieur of Lorraine, sink down to hell!
And in remembrance of those bloody broils,
To which thou didst allure me, being alive,
And here in presence of you all, I swear
I ne'er was King of France until this hour.
This is the traitor that hath spent my gold
In making foreign wars and civil broils.
Did he not draw a sort of English priests
From Douai to the seminary at Rheims,
To hatch forth treason 'gainst their natural queen?
Did he not cause the King of Spain's huge fleet
To threaten England and to menace me?
Did he not injure monsieur that's deceased?
Hath he not made me in the Pope's defence
To spend the treasure that should strength my land
In civil broils between Navarre and me?
Tush, to be short, he meant to make me monk,
Or else to murder me, and so be king.
Let Christian princes that shall hear of this,
(As all the world shall know our Guise is dead)
Rest satisfied with this: that here I swear,
Ne'er was there king of France so yoked as I.

EPERNOUN

My lord, here is his son.

Enter the GUISE'S SON.

HENRY

Boy, look where your father lies.

GUISE'S SON

My father slain! Who hath done this deed?

HENRY

Sirrah, 'twas I that slew him, and will slay
Thee too an thou prove such a traitor.

GUISE'S SON

Art thou king and hast done this bloody deed?
I'll be revenged!
　　　　　　He offereth to throw his dagger.

HENRY

Away to prison with him! I'll clip his wings
Or e'er he pass my hands. Away with him!
　　　　Exit BOY [*guarded*].
But what availeth that this traitor's dead,
When Duke Dumaine, his brother, is alive,
And that young cardinal that is grown so proud?
　　　　[*To the* CAPTAIN OF THE GUARD]
Go to the Governor of Orleans,
And will him, in my name, to kill the duke.
　　　　　[*Exit* CAPTAIN OF THE GUARD.]
　　　　　[*To the* MURDERERS]
Get you away. Strangle the Cardinal.
　　　　　[Exit MURDERERS.]
These two will make one entire duke of Guise,
Especially with our old mother's help.

EPERNOUN

My lord, see where she comes, as if she drooped
To hear these news.

Enter [CATHERINE *the*] QUEEN-MOTHER.

HENRY

And let her droop, my heart is light enough.
Mother, how like you this device of mine?
I slew the Guise because I would be king.

CATHERINE

King? Why, so thou wert before;
Pray God thou be a king now this is done.

HENRY

Nay, he was king and countermanded me,
But now I will be king and rule myself
And make the Guisians stoop that are alive.

CATHERINE

I cannot speak for grief. When thou wast born,
I would that I had murdered thee, my son!
My son? Thou art a changeling, not my son.
I curse thee and exclaim thee miscreant,
Traitor to God and to the realm of France.

HENRY

Cry out, exclaim, howl till thy throat be hoarse.
The Guise is slain, and I rejoice therefore!
And now will I to arms; come Epernoun,
And let her grieve her heart out, if she will.

Exeunt the KING *and* EPERNOUN.

CATHERINE

    Away, leave me alone to meditate.

           [*Exeunt* ATTENDANTS *with the body of the* GUISE]

    Sweet Guise, would he had died, so thou wert here!

    To whom shall I bewray my secrets now,

    Or who will help to build religion?

    The Protestants will glory and insult,

    Wicked Navarre will get the crown of France,

    The popedom cannot stand, all goes to wrack,

    And all for thee, my Guise! What may I do?

    But sorrow seize upon my toiling soul,

    For since the Guise is dead, I will not live.

Exit.

Scene XXII

Enter two [MURDERERS] *dragging in the* CARDINAL.

CARDINAL
Murder me not, I am a cardinal.

FIRST MURDERER
Wert thou the Pope thou mightst not 'scape from us.

CARDINAL
What, will you soil your hands with churchmen's blood?

SECOND MURDERER
Shed your blood? O Lord, no, for we intend to strangle you.

CARDINAL
Then there is no remedy but I must die?

FIRST MURDERER
No remedy, therefore prepare yourself.

CARDINAL
Yet lives My brother Duke Dumaine, and more
To revenge our deaths upon that cursed king,

Upon whose heart may all the Furies gripe,
And with their paws drench his black soul in hell!

FIRST MURDERER

Yours, my Lord Cardinal, you should have said.
Now they strangle him.
So, pluck amaine; he is hard-hearted, therefore pull with violence.
Come take him away.

Exeunt [*with the body*].

SCENE XXIII

Enter DUKE DUMAINE, *reading of a letter, with others.*

DUMAINE
  My noble brother murdered by the king!
  O, what may I do for to revenge thy death?
  The king's alone, it cannot satisfy.
  Sweet duke of Guise, our prop to lean upon,
  Now thou art dead, here is no stay for us.
  I am thy brother, and I'll revenge thy death,
  And root Valois his line from forth of France,
  And beat proud Bourbon to his native home,
  That basely seeks to join with such a king,
  Whose murderous thoughts will be his overthrow.
  He willed the Governor of Orleans, in his name,
  That I with speed should have been put to death;
  But that's prevented, for to end his life,
  And all those traitors to the Church of Rome
  That durst attempt to murder noble Guise.
                    Enter the FRIAR.

FRIAR
  My lord, I come to bring you news, that your brother,

the Cardinal of Lorraine, by the king's consent, is lately strangled unto death.

DUMAINE

My brother Cardinal slain, and I alive?
O words of power to kill a thousand men!
Come, let us away and levy men;
'Tis war that must assuage the tyrant's pride.

FRIAR

My lord, hear me but speak. I am a friar of the order of the Jacobins, that for my conscience sake will kill the king.

DUMAINE

But what doth move thee above the rest to do the deed?

FRIAR

O my lord, I have been a great sinner in my days, and the deed is meritorious.

DUMAINE

But how wilt thou get opportunity?

FRIAR

Tush, my lord, let me alone for that.

DUMAINE.

Friar, come with me, we will go talk more of this within.

Exeunt.

Scene XXIV

Sound drum and trumpets, and enter the KING OF FRANCE, *and* NAVARRE, EPERNOUN, BARTUS, PLESHÉ [*and* ATTENDANTS] *and* SOLDIERS.

HENRY
    Brother of Navarre, I sorrow much
    That ever I was proved your enemy,
    And that the sweet and princely mind you bear
    Was ever troubled with injurious wars.
    I vow, as I am lawful King of France,
    To recompense your reconciled love
    With all the honours and affections
    That ever I vouchsafed my dearest friends.

NAVARRE.
    It is enough if that Navarre may be
    Esteemed faithful to the King of France,
    Whose service he may still command till death.

HENRY
    Thanks to my kingly Brother of Navarre.
    Then here we'll lie before Lutetia walls,

Girting this strumpet coty with our siege,
Till, surfeiting with our afflicting arms,
She cast her hateful stomach to the earth.
                    Enter a MESSENGER.

MESSENGER
    An it please your majesty, here is a friar of the
    order of the Jacobins sent from the President of Paris, that
    craves access unto your grace.

HENRY
    Let him come in.
                    [*Exit* MESSENGER.]
                    Enter FRIAR *with a Letter.*

EPERNOUN [*aside to* KING HENRY]
    I like not this friar's look,
    'Twere not amiss, my lord, if he were searched.

HENRY
    Sweet Epernoun, our friars are holy men
    And will not offer violence to their king
    For all the wealth and treasure of the world.
    Friar, thou dost acknowledge me thy king?

FRIAR
    Ay, my good lord, and will die therein.

HENRY
    Then come thou near, and tell what news thou bring'st.

FRIAR

My lord, the President of Paris greets your grace, and
sends his duty by these speedy lines, humbly craving your
gracious reply.
[*Gives letter*]

HENRY

I'll read them, friar, and then I'll answer thee.

FRIAR

Sancte Jacobus, now have mercy on me!
He stabs the KING *with a knife as he readeth the letter, and
then the* KING *getteth the knife and kills him.*

EPERNOUN

O my lord, let him live a while!

HENRY

No, let the villain die, and feel in hell,
Just torments for his treachery.

NAVARRE

What, is your highness hurt?

HENRY

Yes, Navarre, but not to death I hope.

NAVARRE

God shield your grace from such a sudden death!
Go call a surgeon hither straight.
[*Exit an* ATTENDANT.]

HENRY

    What irreligeous pagans' parts be these

    Of such as hold them of the holy church?

    Take hence that damned villain from my sight.

              [SOLDIERS *remove the* FRIAR*'s body*.]

EPERNOUN

    Ah, had your highness let him live,

    We might have punished him for his deserts!

HENRY

    Sweet Epernoun, all rebels under heaven

    Shall take example by his punishment

    How they bear arms against their sovereign.

    Go call the English agent hither straight.

              [*Exit* SOLDIER.]

    I'll send my sister England news of this,

    And give her warning of her treacherous foes.

              [*Enter a* SURGEON.]

NAVARRE

    Pleaseth your grace to let the surgeon search your wound?

HENRY

    The wound, I warrant ye, is deep, my lord.

    Search, surgeon, and resolve me what thou see'st.

              The SURGEON *searcheth* [*the wound*].

              Enter the ENGLISH AGENT.

    Agent for England, send thy mistress word

    What this detested Jacobin hath done.

    Tell her, for all this, that I hope to live;

Which if I do, the papal monarch goes
To wrack and antichristian kingdom falls.
These bloody hands shall tear his triple crown,
And fire accursed Rome about his ears.
I'll fire his crazed buildings and incense
The papal towers to kiss the holy earth.
Navarre, give me thy hand: I here do swear
To ruinate this wicked church of Rome
That hatcheth up such bloody practices.
And here protest eternal love to thee,
And to the Queen of England especially,
Whom God hath blessed for hating papistry.

NAVARRE

These words revive my thoughts, and comfort me
To see your highness in this virtuous mind.

HENRY

Tell me, surgeon, shall I live?

SURGEON

Alas, my lord, the wound is dangerous,
For you are stricken with a poisoned knife.

HENRY

A poisoned knife! What, shall the French king die
Wounded and poisoned both at once?

EPERNOUN

O that that damned villain were alive again,
That we might kill him with some new-found death!

BARTUS

He died a death too good; the devil of hell torture his
wicked soul!

HENRY

Ah, curse him not sith he is dead.

O, the fatal poison works within my breast.

Tell me, surgeon, and flatter not, may I live?

SURGEON

Alas, my lord, your highness cannot live.

NAVARRE

Surgeon, why say'st thou so? The king may live.

HENRY

O no, Navarre, thou must be King of France.

NAVARRE

Long may you live, and still be King of France.

EPERNOUN

Or else die Epernoun.

HENRY

Sweet Epernoun, thy king must die.

My lords, fight in the quarrel of this valiant prince,

For he is your lawful king and my next heir;

Valois' line ends in my tragedy.

Now let the house of Bourbon wear the crown,

And may it never end in blood, as mine hath done!

Weep not, sweet Navarre, revenge my death.

Ah, Epernoun, is this thy love to me?
Henry thy king wipes off these childish tears,
And bids thee whet thy sword on Sixtus' bones,
That it may keenly slice the Catholics.
He loves me not that sheds most tears,
But he that makes most lavish of his blood.
Fire Paris, where these treacherous rebels lurk.
I die, Navarre, come bear me to my sepulchre.
Salute the Queen of England in my name,
And tell her Henry dies her faithful friend.

> *He dies.*

NAVARRE

Come, lords, take up the body of the king,
That we may see it honourably interred.
And then I vow for to revenge his death
As Rome and all those popish prelates there
Shall curse the time that e'er Navarre was king,
And ruled in France by Henry's fatal death.

> *They march out, with the body of the* KING *lying on four men's shoulders, with a dead march, drawing weapons on the ground.*

6

THE NEW
AUGUSTAN PHASE

Augustus established the state by the double action of turning the Senate from an elite governing entity freely in command into a subservient bureaucracy and by transferring power from it to the Legion. Virgil named the passive and obedient society of Augustus 'imperium sine fine' (Aen. 1. 257-96) an empire without end.

It was to be the identical claim of American Empire once the financial system had taken over power from the political class. The essential deception of the Augustan state – that Empire was really republic because the form of the Senate had been maintained – was identical to that of the modern capitalist state, only the Legion had been replaced by the Bank. The empire without end in its modern form was to be the consumer-state.

Laski, in 'The Pluralistic State':

> "We are learning, as John Stuart Mill pointed out in
> an admirable passage, that 'all the facilities which
> a government enjoys of access to information, all

the means which it possesses of remunerating, and therefore of commanding, the best available talent in the market, are not an equivalent for the one great disadvantage of an inferior interest in the result.' (Principles of Political Economy: Mill Vol. 2. p.181) For we now know that the consequent of that inferior interest is the consistent degradation of freedom."

Laski further raised the crucial issue of the modern age now that war is activated by a non-combatant political class under mass conscription laws.

> "If any state, to take the decisive issue, should choose to embark upon war, in each case there is no a priori rightness about its policy. You and I are part of the leverage by which that policy is ultimately enacted. It therefore becomes a moral duty on our part to examine the foundations of state-action.
>
> The last sin in politics is unthinking acquiescence in important decisions."

In the most important study of Tacitus to emerge in recent years, that of Dr. Holly Haynes of Dartmouth College she quotes as her opening epigraph a phrase of Harold Nicholson's, used I take it, in his work on the Versailles Treaty.

> 'But the true record of what happened will give millions of people an untrue impression of what really happened.'

Dr. Haynes identifies the genius of Tacitus as portraying "the internal logic of an era ignorant of itself." Once the Republic, now destroyed, is presented as the political reality while the Emperor has absolute command yet pretending to symbolic status, the ordinary citizen is living in a world of fantasy yet one with a quotidian reality. If you believe the official reality it means that you are basically insane. Pirandello dramatised the madman as the one who knew the scenario was false yet acted within the pretence that it was true. The Augustan dilemma is the living out of a madness from day to day. It is the dilemma of our modernity. Psychosis has covered itself in the toga of Rome, and then strips bare to expose the primal nudity of Greek democracy.

Lionel Trilling ends his book 'Sincerity and Authenticity' with a remarkably perceptive appreciation of the work of the psycho-analyst Ronald Laing.

"The schizophrenic person characteristically has what Laing calls an 'ontological insecurity', a debility of his sentiment of being…It is the family which is directly responsible for the onto-logical break, the 'divided self' of schizophrenia: Laing is categorical in saying that every case of schizophrenia is to be understood as 'a special strategy that the patient invents in order to live an unliveable situation', which is always a family situation, specifically the demand of parents that one have a self which is not one's true self, that one be what one is not. We may put it that Laing construed schizophrenia as the patient's response to the parental imposition of inauthenticity."

To the modern capitalist, who grasps the Augustan duplicity so dazzlingly analysed in the Tacitean view of the Roman Empire by Holly Haynes, it is clear that our civic reality in society today is itself a structured, socially structured psychosis.

The American state's response to the Laingian critique, so clearly understood by Lionel Trilling, was quite simply to refuse the analytic method and to call on a mass re-assessment of all psychic disturbances, both neurotic and psychotic as being a bio-chemical imbalance imposed by crisis and thus requiring a pharmaceutical re-balance by the application of drug therapies.

In one move the Trotsky-ite doctrine was applied to medicine. The administration of men by individual analysis was replaced by the administration of things, in this situation – chemical things.

7

THE UNDERNEATH I

The world of narrative history which we inherit as the record of events which preceded us is itself a precarious evidence on which we are obliged to make our assumptions on present matters and future possibilities.

Put crudely if history is, mistakenly, taken to be what happened, then it leaves unexamined the people in the events. The proper seeing of the historic demands a lucid examination both of the terrain of happenings and the characters who made it happen.

Laski's magisterial survey of the events both preceding and during the time of the 'Vindiciae' vital though it is to our understanding does not confront the intense life and death conflicts involving those who participated in the events.

The authenticated yet fragmented dramatisation of the central happening at the time of the 'Vindiciae' is an inside job. Marlowe knew, as a professional spy, not only what happened but what at a personal level drove the participants. The event was public but the passions were private. The first record required a historian. The second record required a dramatist.

Look at the device of the master dramatist. In the play 'Hamlet' which, narrates the history of the Prince of Denmark. In order, therefore, to get, as it were, underneath, to expose the true nature of the crime, Hamlet stages a play, thus a play within the play.

Hamlet expresses his historical situation:

'The time is out of joint; O cursèd spite
That ever I was born to set it right!'
(1. 5. 186–7)

Hamlet plans to unmask the criminal by staging a play which will expose the author of the criminal event, that is the murder by Hamlet's uncle of Hamlet's father. He calls the play 'The Mousetrap.'

'The play's the thing
Wherein I'll catch the conscience of the King.'
(3. 1. 539-540)

In Marlowe's disturbingly modern recounting of the actions by the principal characters in the St. Bartholomew's Day Massacre two elements stand out, firstly the sense of urgency and passion with which people behave, and secondly that the forces which drive to the public crime are all intensely private. Indeed one can dare to infer that the private passions are the motor of the social event.

Hamlet says to Horatio: 'Give me that man
That is not passion's slave and I will wear him
In my heart's core — ay, in my heart of heart —
As I do thee.'

At the end of the play all the protagonists are dead. Only Horatio is still alive.

For the next evidence to be presented I am forced to change the grammar of the argument to the personal not as poetry, but rather in the mode of Cicero giving the case.

In the '50s of the last century, as a young dramatist, my play, 'A Masque of Summer' was being presented at the Citizens' Theatre in Glasgow. Its subject was that of a young woman who fell ill without apparent cause. A man appears who says he will cure her by writing a poem for her. That will be the cure. Two friends gave professional counsel, Dr. Joseph Schorstein, a brain surgeon, and Dr. Ronald Laing, the psycho-analyst.

Laing invited me to attend a session of his group of psychiatrists who met together and examined their current cases in depth. Present that evening as one of the group was the dazzlingly gifted analyst, Dr. David Cooper. After his vivid description of his session with a schizophrenic girl and her mother, Ronald asked me if I had any observations to make.

I noted that the clinical description involved only the girl and her mother, but I added there were three persons in the room. The third, the analyst, did not figure in the report. Cooper, I recall, lost his detached manner and turned on me, swearing, and enraged.

They had been scientists, observers at an event.

I was a playwright assisting at a drama.

Now, as noted above, Lionel Trilling recognised the primal claim of Laing laying the blame of madness on the family. In the end of this laying bare it saw the responsibility fell on society, the family being the social witnesses of it.

At the same time the Laingian examination had unmasked the flaw in the psychiatric module. If you like it de-structured the Freudian claim to a scientific basis for his system.

This marks a turning-point in our time. The denial of an enlightenment. Examine it closely. To repeat:

The direct result of the American State's rejecting the Freudian psycho-analytic method was the decision of the political class to base all future diagnostics of mental stress and crisis as having a physiological identity, and thus matching every mental condition to a pharmaceutical treatment. It followed from this that the doctor was obliged to go from symptoms to medication. Narrative was gone, experiencing selfhood was gone. Sick man had become thing requiring other things to restore him to whole thingness.

All during the first phase of Laing's launching his attack on the psychiatric method and profession our close friendship continued. At that time I found that one among our group of British-born Muslims manifested a mental condition which distressed me. I asked Ronald for his guidance. When he found out that the person concerned was the son of Britain's leading psycho-analyst he told me he could not comment as it was unethical. He was psycho-analysing the man's mother. He was, in metaphor, in the Queen's bedroom but behind the arras was only a courtier, Polonius. He was still designing his 'Mousetrap' to kill the King.

The Players named it anti-psychiatry. He succeeded.

8

THE UNDERNEATH II

The dramatic version of what happened is not on a lesser level than the theoretical or political narration of the event, rather the philosophical view is, as it were, beside the point, while the dramatic version reveals what the protagonists hide in their rhetoric and their actions.

The pivotal figure linking the classical era to the modern is Seneca. Seneca faces back in time via Ovid to the Greek culture's way of making sense of event. He also faces forward via the Elizabethan and Jacobean theatre to the modern world's crises. The pivotal modern figure proves to be Marlowe, as a highly conscious political insider, not just as Elizabethan spy but as one of the aristocratic Oxford linked republican, post-christian circle of Essex, Ralegh and the emergent European elite.

Marlowe had translated the erotic Elegies of Ovid and most importantly the first volume of Lucan's republican epic 'Civil War'. He moved in that circle which ordered event not the mass which executed it. In a way which Shakespeare the consummate playwright never could the young Marlowe tasted and aspired to power.

In an important book for political theory, A.J. Boyle writes in 'Tragic Seneca':

> 'All of Shakespeare's great tragic figures are in some sense Tamburlaine, that is to say (Seneca's) Hercules, Medea, Hippolytus, Theseus, Oedipus, Atreus, Thyestes. They create a linguistic world with their self as its referential centre.'

Boyle refers to Seneca's 'Medea' – 'Medea nunc sum', Now I am Medea – as:

> 'The Senecan paradigm of the linguistic base of the Renaissance self, its foundation on the ability to construct and fix itself through and in language.'
> (Tragic Seneca: Boyle p.177)

Marlowe moved in a circle that was by education and choice republican and post-christian. In making Tamburlaine his hero he was projecting a man who proved undefeated in battle, and a world ruler. He is a complex mix of unitarian believer and Renaissance power claiming authority over the world and mankind. Claiming that unlimited authority he reaches beyond Islam and burns the Qur'an only to find the doctors diagnosing mortal death and re-establishing Divine Power. The first Tamburlaine was a triumphant public success but it openly boasted its author's republican views as well as his disdain for the christian power system. He now flaunted a new set of values belonging both to the alien Muslim ethos and Republican Rome.

> 'Your births shall be no blemish to your fame,
> For virtue is the fount whence honour springs.'

(Tamburlaine 1. 4.4. p.127-8)

'Shall give the world to note, for all my birth,
That virtue solely is the sum of glory
And fashions men with true nobility.'
(Tamburlaine 1. V.2 p.125-127)

Virtue is, of course, the Roman moral quality elevated in the Republic, and also the coded morality of chivalry, in itself anti-christian and implicitly republican.

Virtus et summa potestas.
(Lucan: Civil War: 494)

Virtue is incompatible with absolute power.

Marlowe's circle, raised on Seneca, Ovid and Lucan are unmasking the very fundamental rite of the Mass, wine into blood, far from being the act of initiated priests is an ancient one connected to Tiresias and Oedipal crime.

'Genitor, horresco intuens;
libata Bacchi dona permutat cruor.'
(Seneca: Oedipus 323/4: Zwierlein, Oxford)

'Father, I shudder to look at it! The gift
of wine we poured there, changes now into blood.'

Thomas Kyd shared a room with Marlowe and was both influenced by his ideas and affected by his awakening the English language to its Latin inheritance. Look at the beautiful speech of his revenge hero, Hieronimo:

'O eyes, no eyes, but fountains fraught with tears!
O life, no life, but lively form of death!
O world, no world, but mass of public wrongs,
Confused and filled with murder and misdeeds!'
(Spanish Tragedy: Kyd, 3. 2. p.1-4)

In the Arden edition mention is made of the grammatical structure as being built on the rules of Roman rhetoric.

> 'The opening of this monologue presents a large number of rhetorical devices: alliteration (fountains/fraught, life/lively, murder/misdeeds), initial repetition (eyes, life, world), parallelism (the first three lines), syntactical balance at each side of the chiasmus (confused and filled/murder and misdeeds) and oxymoron (lively form of death).'
> (Arden Edition: the Spanish Tragedy. p.112. Bloomsbury)

What is happening in the middle of the Renaissance, with Roman Catholic mondialism dying before the awakened power of Reformation individualism echoing as it did Roman, that is ancient Roman republicanism, is an emergent voice. A voice after silence. Freedom after tyranny. In Kyd's 'Householder's Philosophy' he wrote:

> 'Usury is a corruptor of a Commonwealth, a disobeyer of the Laws of God, a Rebel and resister of all humane orders, injurious to many, the spoil of most of those that most uphold it, only profitable to itself, and more infectious that the pestilence.'

In the Prelude to 'the Spanish Tragedy' he places the usurers in the deepest hell: 'Where usurers are choked with melted gold.' (1. 1. p.67)

Marlowe's famous question: 'Does he not have as good right to Coine as the Queen of England,' today remains unanswered.

Alessandro Schiesaro's 'The Passions in Play' sounding a major theme in his profound study of Seneca's theatre states: 'The words of poetry represent a decisive victory against the repressive morality of silence.'

At the end of 'The Spanish Tragedy' its hero, vengeance finally accomplished, declares:

"Hieronimo
    Now do I applaud what I have acted.
    Nunc iners cadat manus.
    Now to express the rupture of my part.
    First take my tongue and afterward my heart.
    (He bites out his tongue)

King
    Oh, monstrous resolution of a wretch!
    See, Viceroy, he hath bitten forth his tongue
    Rather than reveal what we required.

Castile
    Yet he can write.

King
    And if in this he satisfy us not,
    We will devise th' extremest kind of death
    that ever was invented for a wretch.
    (Then Hieronimo makes signs for a knife to mend his pen)

Castile

Oh he would have a knife to mend his pen.

Viceroy

Here, and advise thee that thou write the truth.

(Hieronimo with a knife stabs the Duke of Castile and himself to death.)

Note that the Latin Phrase 'now let my inactive hand fall' derives from Ovid's 'manus iners'. (Ars Amatoria 2. 706)

Marlowe had opened a door onto a world up until then denied. A world where men took on the full weight of their actions in a present with a now to be confronted past, both memory and the forgotten. In a new encounter with time Marlowe's Faustus calls out:

'O lente, lente currite noctis equi!
The stars move still, time runs, the clock will strike.'

Marlowe has taken the lines addressed by the poet longing for the night in his mistress' arms not to end and raised them to a height of metaphysical sublimity. 'Go slowly, slowly, you horses of the night' (Ovid: Amores 1. 13. 40)

Christianity is finished, but man still lives, but now with new guides to what lies hidden.

OEDIPUS
AND DIONYSUS

Ian Dallas

'Der König Oedipus hat ein
Auge Zuviel vielleicht.'

FRIEDRICH HÖLDERLIN

For
Ernst Jünger

CHARACTERS

In order of appearance

OEDIPUS

PRIEST

CHORUS

CREON

ASTYMEDUSA

TIRESIAS

PELOPS

MAENADS

MESSENGER

DIONYSUS

Oedipus And Dionysus

The Royal Palace at Thebes.
In the centre stand the great double doors which lead inside.
In the middle of the Arena is an altar.
Music. A group of citizens enter.
They sway and dance in an act of supplication and then
they turn before the great doors, waving staffs and beating drums.
The doors swing open.
Enter Oedipus in khiton.
He is majestic and powerful.

OEDIPUS: I am Oedipus. Speak to me. I am yours.

PRIEST: We have sacrificed to Athena.
We have burned incense before Apollo.
We have called on the heavens for mercy –
Nothing has changed. The plague has come.
No sooner does its poison enter the body
Than the sick man must prepare for death.
Throbbing with fever, his blood breaks
From his vein black and fetid, fatal.
No man is safe. Doom is written
For the child unborn, for the fated house.

The air is hard to breathe
The barren soil awaits the dead.
Oh Oedipus King of Thebes
Your adopted city dies in the sunlight.
Help us. You are great. You are chosen.
Strong, noble, guarding a secret,
You came to us. Under tyranny then,
We were broken by taxes, and terror.
The winged cat-woman ruled our days
By a power we could not understand.
Guarded by riddle, sleepless
The Sphinx held Thebes in thrall.
And then you came before her asking,
Fearless, to answer the unknown
Question. Questions that unsolved
Meant your certain death. Oedipus!
You knew the answer then. Give us
The answer now – to this
Our new disaster.

OEDIPUS: No new disaster, but the same.
Life brings its funeral cortege
To the lovers' door. Always
And again our tribulation comes.
This is one story, and the Sphinx
Was but the prelude and the start.
As this city's streets lie putrid
With the infective dead, my mind
In sleep is troubled with dreams.
Dark, dangerous and unexplained.

PRIEST: When the Sphinx's puzzle, a wager
Against your death was set
You did not hesitate or refuse
What goes on four legs, mornings,
Then on two, in sunshine,
But on three under the moon.
You answered, smiling –

CHORUS: Man! The crawling child on fours.
The walking full grown man, and last
The bent and crippled form of age,
As man in his evening, with a stick
Goes three legged to the grave.

OEDIPUS: But I did not say that!

PRIEST: That was your answer, sir.
We sing it every year's end.
Upon your birthday, children too.
We know what freed us, Oedipus.
You broke the Sphinx's power,
With just one word you spoke:
Man! Now, man – speak again.

OEDIPUS: How is it possible that man forgets
So soon the word that sets him free?
I answered what was in my dream.
What I saw dreaming as I lay
Sweating and turning, crying in the night.
I spoke the only truth a man can speak
When I cried out the answer to the Sphinx.
That creature of riddle and three states,

The mortal man, unknown to cities,
Held in thrall before the puzzle – is
ME! Me. Me. Oedipus, the stranger.
This was the word that shrivelled up
And ended the secret power and rule. Ego.
I. For this you made me King.

PRIEST: You rule us, so, irony appeals to you.
Have it your way, we know the story well.
Now we implore you, in our pain,
Do not mock us, or turn your head away,
Or speak of dreams. Speak life. Help!
Guide us – where swift Apollo failed.

OEDIPUS: There is a time when unseen forces
Dominate the day, its actions and its end.
There is a time when dream lays bare
The secrets of a story and its threads
So that the meaning dominates until
The senses all submit and something new,
Utterly new is born on earth. This
Time has come. And freedom's near.

PRIEST: Oedipus. King, man and saviour.
I knew you would not leave us to a plague.
Look – Creon comes, garlanded with news.
   Enter Creon.

CREON: Oedipus – I come from Delphi.
I have placed my hand upon the centre
Of the world, and heard the Oracle.
Touch me and be purified. I've news.

OEDIPUS: I do not need to touch you, Creon.
Your state shines out. I see quite well.
Give us your good news. My dream begins.

CREON: Dream, why speak of dreams
when oracles explain?
The path to health lies open to us now.
The Oracle has shown the way. Shall we?

OEDIPUS: No, speak before the people. The plague
Has brought great suffering and they wait
For news to break the curse on Thebes.

CREON: I have it then. People of Thebes! Apollo
    spoke.
There is a cancer in the land. A man. A sickness.
Cast him out. Exile the killer. Free the state.
A King was killed. A double, triple crime behind
Lies in the shadows. Find him out. This
The Apollonian word of wisdom for the Theban mass.

OEDIPUS: It all coheres.
The trap has sprung. Oedipus
Has been picked to take upon himself – disaster!
I will not walk into my dream. I want to know.
I'll bring this terror under the sun.
Till all can see – and understand.

PRIEST: Oedipus has spoken. He will find the killer –
Expose him and cast him out.

OEDIPUS: Even if he should be immortal and a god.
I swear.

CREON: What do you swear, Oedipus? Riddles
Have become your obsession and your game.

OEDIPUS: I say the Oracle spoke the truth.
Now we must unveil the hidden story
That destroys the city and drives you
To the gods for guidance. You
Whose only desire is for my crown.
There is no doubt – the Oracle spoke
The truth – the truth of Creon,
Who wants to see my downfall.

CREON: Who was the King and who the killer?
That is my question now.
I will bring the blind one to you.
Who can see what is hidden and speak
What men do not dare to think.
Why, Oedipus! I think you've lost
Your taste for riddles and the truth.
    Exit Creon.

OEDIPUS: People of Thebes, Priest of Zeus.
Go home. Tell the city it is time.
Soon we will have unravelled the rope
That strangles life in Thebes.
You have my royal promise. Go.
There is no fear that knowledge
And remembering cannot cure.
    The crowd leave.
    Through the palace door rushes Oedipus' wife,
    Astymedusa.
    They embrace.

ASTYMEDUSA: I heard Lord Creon's words.
From the day you came to Thebes
He has envied you life, and me.
He will not rest until the throne
And all the state is in his hands.

OEDIPUS: Yet he is not my enemy. Come close.
My dearest wife, it's you they want,
My sons, my daughters, all our house.
But why? Who is my enemy? And what?
What is the golden cup they want?
With your most royal name – Astymedusa
You were no prize given to me
For saving Thebes. Pelop's daughter
Was sent to me by a King.
And you came to me, choosing and desiring.
Free and fierce in love I found you.
As I find you still, my best companion,
Passionate friend, dearer to me than all.
They will not take you from me,
Nor destroy my children, and yet –

ASTYMEDUSA: And yet, and yet. Don't turn away.
You cannot hide from me, husband.
I am your truth, your mirror. Friend!
How can you tell yourself and not
Tell me?

OEDIPUS: Fear, a long dark dragon in the night.

ASTYMEDUSA: Describe it to me. Let us look.
It's daylight now. Like what?

OEDIPUS: It is the labyrinth of Minos.
And then another hidden one.
And then a form obscure, cold
And inescapable. It is as if
Here are men and women, passions,
Plague and death. And yet,
Moving and thrusting into time lie
Ancient cthonic powers that force
Us into acts we do not understand.
It is as if soon we will have done
What we did not do. Spoken
What never came from silence.
It is as if — as if —

ASTYMEDUSA: As if?

OEDIPUS: Freedom were only running and
Olympic games. Astymedusa.
I have to find out but what if —

ASTYMEDUSA: You have told me nothing only
Fear, as if, what if. Speak.
Has nothing come to you in dreams?

OEDIPUS: Something most strange, like sky
In an eclipse, making day moonlight.
A dream, yes, but behind it history.
Our lives. I can tell you now.
Polybus, King of Corinth, and Merope.
These were my parents, so I thought.
Once in a night of feasting, a prince,
Drunk and in anger, cursed me.

I was a bastard from another house.
Disturbed I asked my sweet parents
Tell me, please, the truth.
No, no, they insisted, all is well.
The man was lying, drunk.
Still troubled in my heart I went
Out from my Corinthian home
Until I came to Delphi.
There Apollo turned, the far-striking,
And struck at me.

ASTYMEDUSA: Apollo. Of course. Apollo.

OEDIPUS: You will marry your mother, breed
Your children by her, kill your father
And be the scandal of the world.
Spill your father's blood and stir
The mother's, making a family
With a triple curse.
And so I ran. And ran.
Until my strong straight feet
Were red with blood. Corinth
My childhood home lay far away.
Then in a deep valley, green
With oak trees and the vine
I came upon a princely caravan.
Bandits had killed the men,
Left none alive, or so it seemed.
Then a hand moved, and clutched,
As if to save, a royal sceptre.
I took him in my arms, and helped him,

Dying, and sublime before his end.
He looked at me. He smiled. Touched
My lips, and said: I know you.
Know yourself as they command,
And you'll be safe. Forgive me.
I broke my pledge. They set the trap.
But see! Somewhere a god is moving.
I have looked upon you.
On that he died, smiling. It was him.

ASTYMEDUSA: Laius. Your true father and the King.

OEDIPUS: Yes. I buried him and travelled on.
Polybus and Merope sought me out.
Told me the truth, or part of it,
Wept and went away. He broke some
Sacred, ancient pact that binds
Men with men in power and rule.
To save his punishment from me.
He sent me to the hills away
From the reach of Furies and of men.
Until, fleeing Apollo's words
And curse, I fell exhausted
Into the valley of my fate
Where three roads meet.

ASTYMEDUSA: I begin to see day by daylight.
Yes. Three roads meet here.
Ancient. Paths which take us
To the sacred groves of war, manhood,
And the rites of power. Here
The sceptre rules, the phallus

And the sword. Oedipus,
If we are to emerge alive, knowing,
We must go back in time, forward, too.
Before this matter ends, it may be
That we must drag the divinities
Out from their hidden hills,
The sanctuaries made pure
By burning entrails and the dance
Of virgins' feet. Oedipus.
Will you fight on the foothills
Of Olympus, take on Apollo?

OEDIPUS: You see Apollo, the far-striking
As the one who has marked us
And hunts us down. I do not care.
I can only live free, pursuing the truth.
This is my glory and my name.
I can plead against Apollo,
But not against disgrace
And an incest I never knew.
Laius is dead, not by my hand.
Jocasta is elsewhere, too old
To bear a brood by any man,
Poor mother that I never knew.
Polybus and Merope are to me
Father and mother. Would I kill him,
Wed her. That's crime. This,
A trap. There may be no escape.

ASTYMEDUSA: No. We will unknot the knotted,
Count them one by one to read

The pattern of this tapestry.
My mother, Hippodamia, knew
What lies behind these things.
When, playing at her knee, spinning,
She used to talk of another world
Of heroes, Titans, supermen.
Pelops, my father she named the last
Of the initiates of the gods.
In those days boys came to manhood
In the Andreia of the gods
Servant lovers they were passed
Through test and terror until
Their lord declared them men,
Sons were sent to other lands
To come back, brutal, fearless
Burned, by the knowledge of being man.
Themselves possessed, they learned
Possession, tenderness with women.
The line was crossed, and they
Returned, taught warriors ready
To pass on in turn the initiation
Of what made a hero wild and free.
Poseidon was the fierce lover of Pelops.
And the test he set him changed the world.
To win my mother's hand a chariot race
Was set upon the Olympic plain.
His rival, Oenomaos, had taken
Myrtilus as his driver, the best
Of all the riders in the land.
That night Poseidon guided him to cunning.
He rose and greased the axelpin

Dooming Myrtilus to a tragic fall.
Poseidon's beloved Pelops won
And gave me life by Hippodamia.
So it was that when another chosen
Charioteer came to us from Thebes
Pelops appointed him tutor
Teacher of my brother, Chrysippus.
Laius loved him in a way of heroes
With this ferocious tender love
That brings men into manhood.
When Laius left for Thebes with him
He took a promise of a bride
That when he had a son, Pelop's
Daughter would be sent to him.
And so I came to you in Thebes,
That very year you saved the city.
I learned one other thing.
My mother told me Laius was the last
Hero to initiate to manhood.
That after him an age was gone
And the line withdrawn and men
Would move closer to women
And what had made men wild would
Make them soft and time
Cause fear until we learned
To count the days and years.
Apollo cast an Oracle on Thebes:
Build a shrine to the Furies
Of Oedipus and Laius, for
Their children will not survive.

OEDIPUS: You knew. Four children
And you never spoke.

ASTYMEDUSA: I am a hero's daughter
And I do not count the days.
I live for life, and you and now.
But Apollo the far-striking
Has aimed at the Aegidae of Oedipus.
He is the god of health
He is the sender of plagues.
All these Oracles, this sickness
On the city, come from him.
But why? To what end, Apollo?
Are you not lord of order, civic harmony?

OEDIPUS: With the wisdom of innocence
We will reach the well and drink
Of this knowledge. Come.
Let us go in and plan a path.

ASTYMEDUSA: I hold a papyrus that Hermes
Got from Zeus, by it the dead
Will speak and tell their tale.
Pelops must know this thing
Right at its heart, some ancient
Some unfinished feud. Oedipus,
We'll breath pure air again.
> *As they go to the palace the chorus enters in*
> *black, carrying corpses led by the priest.*
> *The cortege stops as do the royal couple.*
> *They stare at each other as the drums beat, then*
> *Oedipus and Astymedusa enter the palace.*

PRIEST: There is no plague within.
Inside the palace gates they're safe.
This miasma like the mist
Covers the city. All is dark.
Look! Inside are lights. Music.
Perhaps our suffering comes from there.
It may be some ancient magic
From Olympia brought by the wife
Of Oedipus. He is no more
The glorious hero we once knew.

CHORUS: Our sons are dead. Our daughters too.
The stench of burning corpses scent
The avenues of Thebes where once
Among its trees the white doves flew.
Young lovers' songs are silent now.
The old are dumb with grief
As one vast pain gives out its cry.
We have a King who does not care.
The Oracle spoke. Find out the man
Who killed a King. What King —
Within our lands — it must mean that.
Creon has called on Oedipus
We call on him, in grief, dying
Help this city of gravediggers.

PRIEST: No ruler can carry the people's pain.
One day you are at their coronation
Crown them with laurel leaves
Apollo's darlings, young and fair.
Next day they call us to the long war

We listen to the lists of dead
Then by the cenotaph we stand
In a cold winter, huddled,
Tears frozen on the widows' cheeks,
Watching the leader lay his wreath
And crown, in honour of our dead
Mourning a generation gone.
Then he walks in his warm halls
Planning new taxes for the spring.

CHORUS: He is the stranger, other blood.
He is the ruler, we the ruled.
The earth has parted between us.
Thrones topple, kings die, people
Continue. We go on. Power.
Real power lies with us.
Generation is our sceptre.
Numbers our crown, and movement
In the mass our sword.
In our need he spoke a word,
Now Creon stretches out his hand.
His time has come and we accept
That he may wave to us as once
King Oedipus, smiling, waved
From high balconies to us below.

PRIEST: Look! A boy leads blind Tiresias
To confront the King. Creon
Has made his move for Thebes.
    Enter a boy leading Tiresias,
    who walks with a staff.

TIRESIAS: Beat twice upon the door.
Now, leave me with the King.
    They leave.
    The palace door opens and Oedipus enters.
I did not want to come. Grant
And I'll take my leave to go.

OEDIPUS: Sir, you are a seer of the unseen.
You know the hidden secrets
You make plain the Pythian codes
Here is a knot I need to see
Untied or cut, to set me free.

TIRESIAS: I know exactly what it is.
I have understood. Obey.
Take my advice, great King.
Play your part. Submit. Accept.
Bow down before the deed of time.
History is emerging. Look.
All the pieces move. Rules
Must be allowed to rule. But you
Resist, struggling against the tide.
Oedipus, play your part
As I can promise immortality,
Suffering now, and then a name,
And a whole world's pity on you.
A glorious old age, crowned
In Colonus by sanctity.
Like me. Blind – and all-wise.

OEDIPUS: This is a worthless fame to me.

TIRESIAS: You fool! The gods will silence you.
Would you unweave the woven cloth?
Wipe out the painter's line, the vase
Left blank without a tale to tell.
This is your last chance in time.
Accept that you are Oedipus.

OEDIPUS: I am Oedipus. True to myself.
You know that I will know and speak.
You must speak out – and tell the truth.

TIRESIAS: I have no choice: Oedipus. It is you.
You are the curse, the volcano
From which this lava flows. Thebes
Lies dying at your hand, my King.

OEDIPUS: Go on. Speak and be clear.

TIRESIAS: You are the murderer of the King.

OEDIPUS: I have killed no King. No harm
Can come on me. You, Tiresias,
Can do me no harm.

TIRESIAS: No. You will be struck by a god.
Far-striking and implacable.

OEDIPUS: This is Creon, plotting. The throne
Of Thebes – this is the purpose.
You work for Creon's rule.

TIRESIAS: No. This is a greater matter
Than a King. I serve Apollo.
I can do nothing for you now.

OEDIPUS: As you did nothing for yourself.
You have bowed the head, and hate
That I raise mine to knowledge, growth
For all the human family. You,
Tiresias are blind. Alone,
Reading bird's entrails in the dark.
Womanless, unloved, unkissed.

TIRESIAS: Silence! I see. You are blind.
Thebes will love me, garland me,
You are the guilty one. Shout it!
There is no secret now. You killed
The King.

OEDIPUS: What King? Name this victim!

TIRESIAS: He has been identified. The King
Was Laius, son of Labdacos.
Soon his murderer will be exposed
Before the people. He had eyes.
He will be blind. He was rich.
He will be poor. He will leave
A beggar with stick tapping his way.
Killer of his father, to his mother,
Son and husband.

OEDIPUS: Oh monstrous, monstrous lie!
How can you serve a god who lies?
I'll prove my innocence, I promise.

TIRESIAS: How? Can the stones speak for you
In your defence? Oedipus.

You cannot bear this knowledge.
One day you'll seek me out and say:
Tiresias wise man, it's better
To be blind. Solve the riddle,
And prepare for fame, poor man.

Tiresias turns and goes with his servant
At the same time the chorus return.

CHORUS: We are disturbed, confused, anxious.
The wind has not lifted. Plague
Still sweeps the city, families die.
We are afraid of the water, the air,
The houses' walls. Help us.

OEDIPUS: People of Thebes, I need you now.
Forces I have not faced, and cannot
Name or point to – seek me out.
Sometimes I think it's Creon.
At other times a god, yet why?
Are not the gods just and good?

CHORUS: Do not speak these things. Never
Doubt the gods' power or down
Like thunder from Olympus
They will roar, destroying us,
Our city and our fate.

OEDIPUS: Is that not what happens now?
Can you not see how all things
Move and conspire to punish me?
If I lose this battle
You too, will come down with me,

Into a long darkness already
Prepared and chosen. And yet –
It need not be. If we
Together ask for truth to speak
Clear in the sunlight, Zeus,
Who fought for justice will,
I know, at last speak for us.

CHORUS: What are you asking us?

OEDIPUS: Work with me. Think for yourselves.
Together we can solve the riddle.

CHORUS: Do we not suffer enough? Are we heroes?
It is your job to solve riddles.
You are Oedipus, the knower, the diviner.
We cannot think about these things.
We are, already, too busy about our lives.
We are uneasy as it is, unsure.
Our house is full of riddles unsolved.
There are questions whispering
In corridors, glances so strange
Upon the stairs. Our wives dream
Strange dreams of barbarians
Who rape, attack and kill.
Our daughters rouse us when
By chance we touch, thighs
Responding, against nature.
Our sons linger in kitchens
Cooking while we ride to hound.
We are busy living. Interruptions –
Frighten us. You see, we need

Someone to blame. Someone to take
All this ordinary anxiety, called
Morning, and pay for it.
Pay with his life. Take all
The filth that is our family life
And shame of dust on surfaces
And wash it clean with blood.
Punish our women for that look
Of tenderness, and silence
Forever the tenor voices
Of our sons.

OEDIPUS: You've chosen me – to pay.

CHORUS: Oh no. my Lord. Not you.
The guilty one – whoever he may be.

OEDIPUS: Creon has done this thing.
It must be him. He wants the throne.

CHORUS: Please understand one thing. We are
Too troubled in our homes
To care of plots in palaces.
We are fully occupied with pain.
We are sure the authorities in time
Will reveal the guilty party
Punish him and let us all return
To the normality that waits for us
Quick intercourse on clean sheets,
Taxation, doctors in attendance
When we die. King Oedipus
Tonight we will know.

OEDIPUS: Yes. I swear I will know
Before the dawn. Leave me.
Leave me! I order you to go.
  The chorus cringe before him.
  They leave.
  Enter Astymedusa.

ASTYMEDUSA: Ssh! The sun goes down.
See there on the horizon
The two horns of the bull.
At the moment the sun dips
Down to lie between the horns
He will appear, my dear father,
Pelops, whose greatness is to come.
Is that not his tall figure
Striding? Father, speak.

OEDIPUS: It is the watchman of the night.

ASTYMEDUSA: Here. Here he comes, the sun
Lies on the earth's edge. See.
Oh dear, my father, seeing you
The years roll back, I want
To play again, look up to you.
  Pelops wrapped in a great cloak appears.

PELOPS: Daughter. Do not approach the dead.
I slept but you have called me
By an ancient call. Zeus I obey
And his word comes to me. Why
Call me from the blessed shore,
Why ferry me again across
The dark and icy river?

ASTYMEDUSA: You sent me to Laius' son as bride.
Now Apollo with great rage sets
Slavering hounds of fate upon him.
Oedipus seeks knowledge.
Who is his enemy? What word
Will liberate him from a doom
Of lies, false incest, accused
Patricide, an eternal shame?

PELOPS: Oedipus. Your father loved my son
And brought him into the ranks
Of warrior power. As erastes
He held the sacred door to man.
There, in the Andreia of the gods,
Under his secret oath of strength
Marriage, and intercourse, and home
Are things forbidden. Yet one night
Against Apollo's order to him
Not to lie with women, procreate,
Until his term as hero-maker
Had set him free, in drunken joy
He took Jocasta to his bed.
And you were his forbidden child.

OEDIPUS: Then is this punishment on me
That I exist? Is innocence
To be destroyed by gods
Who rule by justice under Zeus?

PELOPS: My time is short, see how the sun
Dips and disappears. The past

You know. Now know the future.
My line has gone to Atreus.
By his house will my name be known.
And Atreus' son will be a king.
Whose name will last till the earth dies.
Agamemnon. Hero of war,
Victim of peace. Theme
Of the world's song forever.
Yet for his awful death,
There can be no escape. Zeus.
Destiny, and the mist-walking
Erynys, will accomplish this.
Murdered by his wife's lover,
She in turn killed by her own son.
Orestes. Orestes, for the murder
Of this mother will be driven
Mad with terror, unable to be free
Of the haunting Furies
That will await him
Upon every bridge, behind each door.
Until, at last, worn out
Defeated and distraught – Athena
Takes him in. Justice
Will be set up – for him.
From his crime, by vast compassion
Athena will decree the courts
Of Law for all the city.
This is the end and purpose
Of our pain.

OEDIPUS: I do not understand. Why me?
If the House of Pelops' Atreus
Is doomed to make Athena mighty,
What has this to do with Laius' son,
The House of Labdacos?

PELOPS: I will speak one word to you.
Think. Your life depends on it
Although your name is doomed.
Fit the pieces together.
You are still the riddle-master.
Where was my error made?
Poseidon, the Trident Lord
Of raging tides and ocean depths,
Defend me. What was his ancient
Enmity with wise Athena and why
Place Pelops at its heart?
He was the guardian of us all –
The Aegidae, your House, and mine
The Atridae. This matter
Does not lie with the high lords
Of Mount Olympus. You touch
The deepest truths of time
And man. Beyond the family
Of blood and tribal ties
A new age has begun
Founded upon other rules
A new religion and its sacrifice.
Yet all this is held in place
By ancient ropes that bind.
Hidden within the Delphic Temple

Lies a sacred grove
There Atreus' son will sacrifice
To save our House which I
Made famous by a chariot-race
Pleasing to Poseidon and to me.
When I won, who lost? Whose anger
Fell upon the Atridae?
This story does not end
Upon the icy crags where Zeus
Decrees, but deep in the forest
Tangled in black ivy
Where women laughing drink
Their children's blood
With power and laughter
That make Olympus shake.

ASTYMEDUSA: He fades. He disappears. Father!
Speak the name to Oedipus.

PELOPS: Reach out and drink the wine.
He turns fading in the darkness and disappears.

OEDIPUS: Reach out and drink the wine?
Who was it that he threw
Into the dust that day
Upon the Olympic plain?

ASTYMEDUSA: Oenamaos was his name.

OEDIPUS: He who desires the wine.

ASTYMEDUSA: King Oenamaos therefore
Was a servant of the god —

OEDIPUS: Dionysus!

ASTYMEDUSA: Dionysus!

OEDIPUS: Dionysus Kadmeios.
Right here in Thebes the homeless
God declares his home. Seven
Gates keep out the stranger
But through them all at once
The dancing god Dionysus
Yearly makes his triumph.
With this we plunge dizzily
Into the depth of night
And moon dancing, and
Maenads whirling in a circle.
Yet we must speak with him.
Call him, whatever the price,
To know at last –

ASTYMEDUSA: Oedipus. Years ago,
At Hippodamia's side,
When blood first flowed from me,
And all the rites of womanhood
Were done, I learned another art.
My mother took me to the forest
Of the pine and there
Within a grove, all lit by flares
I joined the swaying circle
Of the maenads. Placed
In the centre of the holy ring
I drank the undiluted wine
Of madness, blood and ecstasy.

Oedipus. I am his servant.
His handmaiden stands before you.
This is the time – now –
That we can call him into
Presence. Dionysus Lysios.
By this name he will speak to us.
The god who releases –
Only he now can set you free.
Let me gather the maenads
To invoke his untamed power
But once called up, Oedipus,
I tell you, by that blood
That flows in me mixed
With his wine, his word
Will be unchangeable.

    OEDIPUS: I have no choice, Astymedusa.
Apollo's arrows have already
Shot from his bow and reached
My heart. Invoke the god.
    Exit Astymedusa
All prayer goes to the Great god.
All supplication soars beyond
The burning meat of sacrifice,
Crossing the invisible line
Of destiny and the decree
Which inescapable lies
Unwoven between the warp
And woof of human pain.
Here I stand, knowing –
Oedipus, on my own feet, free.

I will not be doomed, driven,
Hurled over the cliff
Into an ocean of lies
Victim of Apollo's great
Design. Here I stand.
Enter a messenger.

MESSENGER: My Lord Oedipus,
I come from Creon's Court.
He has declared upon investigation
That you are the killer
Of your own dear father,
Laius the King. A witness
Has declared he found you
Burying the royal body
In a Corinthian wood.
He has declared to the city,
That the Lady Jocasta now
In exile, bore you two sons,
Two daughters. Yet you are
Her child by the dead Laius.
Thus the cause of all the plagues
That wither up the soil of Thebes
Is none other than its mighty King,
Oedipus, the riddle-master,
Destroyer of the Sphinx.
He has despatched a royal guard
To bear the news of who you are
So that Jocasta understand
She lay with her own son,
And husband's murderer.

Creon awaits the confirmation
Of the lady's part in this.
If it be as all expect,
Creon, Tiresias, and the Priests,
Then he will order that you go
Out by the Stranger's Gate
That leads to exile and oblivion.
He asked me to tell you this.
And say, kill not the messenger,
Now that the message lives.

OEDIPUS: Here comes my wife, and her women.
What happens now is dangerous to see.
Agave tore her son Pentheus
Rending his flesh because
He stayed to watch the maenad's dance.
Why is it Thebes which ties
The mother to the son in an
Encounter which must end in death?
We may yet find out.

> The messenger flees as the maenads enter with Astymedusa.
> The maenads carry on high a tray which is a garlanded
> Omphalos.
> They place it on the central altar.
> Oedipus goes to the palace doors and watches from there.
> Astymedusa and the maenads are all dressed alike,
> except that they are in white while her robes are in rich crimson.
> To their music of flutes, drums and chanting they begin
> their evocation of the god.
> In the first part of the dance Astymedusa stands over
> the Omphalos with the women in a half circle before

her, backs to the public.
As the first climax of invocation reaches its high point in
the wild cries of 'Evoe! Evoe! Evoe!' Astymedusa raises
her hands high over her head.
There is an immediate silence.

ASTYMEDUSA: Dionysus! Dionysus!
Here in the City of Seven Gates
Homeless, you have made your home.
Here you made King Kadmos mad,
Founder of the city, broken,
You drove him to smash the stone
And sacred altar of the god.
Twice born intoxicator
Give the sign that sets us free.
Olympic majesty decreed for us
The place of victim in the rites
Weak woman, vestal virgin,
Abandoned sacrificial meat.
Dionysus! Dionysus!
Raise us your maenads
To the singing, swooning peace.
Give the obsidian knife to us
Appoint us your nymphs and nurses
Blood-soaked and lunatic
Laughing and after so much pain –
Mad, mad, mad at last!
We have woven ivy for your crown
We are sticky with the resin of the pine
By our crushing of the grapes
Makes us drunk with an eternal wine!

MAENADS, *as they begin to dance:* We have
woven ivy for your crown
We are sticky with the resin of the pine
By our crushing of the grapes
Make us drunk with an eternal wine!

> *Astymedusa joins in the dance.*
> *It increases in frenzy and speed towards sexual climax.*
> *At the highest point of tension the woman freeze*
> *like statues.*
> *The terrible noise ceases abruptly.*

ASTYMEDUSA: Oh deathly quiet pandemonium!
He – is – here!

> *Down from the back of the auditorium strides Dionysus.*
> *He is crowned with an ivy wreath.*
> *A cloak drapes his naked body covering one*
> *shoulder and tucked into a waist-belt across his muscular thighs.*
> *He beams triumphantly at his women.*
> *He goes to the altar and pours wine into a crater.*
> *He holds it to the lips of Astymedusa.*
> *She drinks*
> *He signals the women.*
> *They retreat to the sides each taking up the thyrsus*
> *which he touches as they pass him.*
> *He motions to Oedipus to come forward. Oedipus*
> *walks gravely to him.*
> *Bows.*

DIONYSUS: I am not here, exactly.
Because I do not have hereness
Or thereness – let us say

I seem to be here – the women
Called on me and I cannot
Resist the rubbing of thighs.

OEDIPUS: Great God –

DIONYSUS: I am not the Great God
Nor, need I say, are that gang
On Olympus, though truly, Zeus,
Is pointing that way. We,
Are the field-force of the stars
The streaming energy of atoms;
The emergent primal shapes,
The great design, and,
The Others represent
A kind of glorious display
Of how mankind may live
Poised between freedom
And the inescapable decree.
Oedipus, I know why
You sent for me – and so
Let me tell you this –
You are not a tragic figure
Broken on the wheel of fate,
But you are the most
Unfortunate of men.

OEDIPUS: Dionysus, Lord of the world's
Madness – help me.

DIONYSUS: Then have a drink. Three cups
For the wise. The first – health.

The second – love. Third – sleep.
Then you should lie down.
For the fourth makes insults.
With the fifth you start to cry.
The sixth and you laugh again.
But the seventh means a fight.
The eighth – the money goes.
The ninth will strike your liver,
But the tenth is mine, my friend
The tenth is madness and it makes
Men – fall.
You are in a trap and you want
To get out of the trap and I
Am to tell you how. Is that it?

OEDIPUS: I am not afraid. I must know.

DIONYSUS: Wisdom is not popular on Olympus
It makes them look so stupid.
Men like it even less. This is,
Precisely, the mess you are in.
Is it not clear to you?
Did Pelops not explain it?
You are not a destiny, sir,
You are a creature about
To become a myth. A necessary
Inescapable – legend.
You are needed –

OEDIPUS: Why? Tell me why!

DIONYSUS: In order that the State continue.

Without you – or – this
Trapped knot of creatures
States could not last the night.
Your crime, your fight, your shame
Make cities, states and empires –
Stand! The murdered father.
The disgraced mother.
The ritual destruction
Of the daughters and the sons
And in the middle – the great
And gifted man, unjustly trapped.
The House of Oedipus – as planned
Is nothing other than a recipe
For social stability and peace…
Which of course means, usury,
Corruption, tyranny, torture,
And a world enslaved.

OEDIPUS: This is the world you want?

DIONYSUS: No, no. Apollo's plan.
But it did not start here.
There was an ancient fight –
Athena and Poseidon. The Trident
Lord loves chaos, and the waves.
When things get hot for me
He always lets me hide out there
In a cave, much nicer than a temple.
Poseidon's son – Theseus
Abandoned the radiant Ariadne
On Naxos, if you recall.
My Ariadne, my beloved,

Rejected and insulted
Because he had a task to do.
Create the city of Athens
Between the ocean and the olive
Or let us say, between
Poseidon and Athena.
So the humans huddle together
Poised between order and chaos.
You see, we are all in it.

OEDIPUS: But what are you doing to me?
Why do you torment my wife,
Plan to destroy my children,
Ruin my name? Do I not rule?
Am I not King? Did I not break
The Sphinx's terror?

DIONYSUS: It is time you looked at things
The way they were and not the way
They tell it in the market place.
The Sphinx was sent by me.
Tiresias, although from Delphi
Is an initiate lord of mine.

OEDIPUS: Then it is you and not Apollo
Who wants my downfall.

DIONYSUS: We work together.
That's how it is.
We do what we can
You do what you like –
Within the rules that is.

OEDIPUS: I wanted to know. All life long
I have sought to understand.
So in your game – tell me
What is your plan for me?

DIONYSUS: It's more or less settled.
You need not worry, from the life
Point of view, you are not affected.
But the people – what they get
Is this: you killed your father.
You married your mother, had
Four children by her, doomed,
In their turn. She hangs herself,
Shamed, you in horror –
I'm sorry about this –
You gouge out your eyes –
And go blind into exile.
Your children of course
One by one in different ways,
I won't depress you with the details,
Get killed, but you,
And Tiresias did try to reassure you,
End up in a sacred grove.
There under the oaks
At Colonus you find peace
And at last serenity.
There you take upon yourself
The title and the crown.
Guardian of Athens.

OEDIPUS: Guardian of Athens!
Like Agamemnon's son,
Like haunted, tired Orestes.
I see it now.

DIONYSUS: You have an eye too many,
My dear. That's dangerous.

OEDIPUS: We are so caught
Within the circle of our hate,
Killing and being killed,
Loving and hating the close
Warm bodies of the family
Fireside and its beds
That power goes on its way
And builds great temples
Plans highways, viaducts,
Gets the world ready
For the road ahead
Promising an absent future
On our present crime.
Was it always this?

DIONYSUS: Oh no. Not like that at all.
We were so happy in the hills.
Tearing limb from limb, dancing
A now unbearable ecstasy, singing
A now unsingable song. We had
Heroes, wild women, blind poets.
Then the cities came, the states.
Just to make it a bit brighter

I'm going to give them theatre.
You – well, the official you.
They will love it. The blinding
And the blood particularly.
The real story – they simply –
And this is hard for you –
Would not be able to confront.
You are their licence never
To be free and never
To destroy the tyrant state.

OEDIPUS: Man must wake up! His enemy
Is himself – the state is
But his mirror. Dionysus,
I beg of you, by your wine,
By your ecstasy, by your wild
And dancing maenads, can you,
The spurting, bubbling, erupting
Lord of madness not let loose
Destruction on the world's states?

DIONYSUS: Apollo is my brother,
Don't forget. However
I'll do you a special little
Favour, just for you.
I have a Queen disciple coming
Who will spend her nights in orgy
Calling on my power, marrying
A king. Their son – Apollo
Will love him, beautiful,
Always making new cities,

I'll model him on you.
They'll say he loved his mother,
Killed the king. I'll turn him
Loose on Great Apollo's Thebes
And let him smash it stone by stone.
We'll call him – Alexander!
What do you say to that?

OEDIPUS: I say you laugh at something
Worse than tragedy.
This cannot be the end.

DIONYSUS: My dear Oedipus. It's only a lie.

OEDIPUS: There must be more,
Something must come
After Dionysus.

DIONYSUS: Beware. We blinded Tiresias
For just this kind of talk
Once he found out. And look at him.
He is blind. At least you live out
Your days in Thebes. A king.
Funeral Games will be held
In your honour. Only the future
Gets to know the lie. Rogues
Will make of your dilemma
A new religion of fear
And dark obedience to man's
Guilt and ignorance. So,
Please accept your place.
The tapestry is complete!

OEDIPUS, *enraged*: I pray out beyond the gods,
Past you and blood stained
Orgies in the hills, past
Zeus, as lightning and as lord,
Past the mist-walking Erynys,
Beyond what can be described,
I call on that power that moves
Whirling stars, and targets
Man to a destiny of time –
Bring to a world enslaved
A people ready to destroy
The State at last, and set
Us free to live – out from
The fatal curse of family –
A man and woman hand in hand
Walking in sunlight
Under tall trees.

DIONYSUS: But that would be the end.

OEDIPUS: Then let it come.

Oedipus holds out his hand to Astymedusa and together they walk back into the palace, looking at each other, smiling. As they do there comes a terrible cry of agony from within the palace. Out of the palace gate an identical figure staggers forward, his gouged eyes two circles of flowing blood. The couple pass him, oblivious to his presence. Triumphantly Dionysus holds out a hand as if to usher him before the audience.

THE END

'The specific character of myth seems to lie neither in the structure nor in the content of a tale, but in the use to which it is put:

And this would be my final thesis:

MYTH IS A TRADITIONAL TALE WITH SECONDARY, PARTIAL REFERENCE TO SOMETHING OF COLLECTIVE IMPORTANCE.'

Walter Burkert

9

NOTA BENE I

At this point an important cultural factor demands attention. The current world situation can openly be seen to have avoided, indeed denied, all political discourse. Something that had continued through wars and frontier re-drawings over the last 600 years has, following World War II, come to an end. Prior to that war political theory and applications were both vibrant and torn with dissent and dialectic. The twentieth century was all political discourse, fascist, socialist and liberal. Half way through the century war stopped. After it a new society emerged, politically undefined and economically already determinist.

In the second half of the century the political class in government step by step lost power. Having achieved universal franchise at the same time they surrendered fiduciary authority. Gaining mass vote and open elections at the same time they handed over finance to an unelected elite of commodity and banking wealth. It was done smoothly, brilliantly inside the liberal module. The French in full colonial crisis were assured a statesman President who could solve it, only condition being that he accept an unelected Prime Minister, employee and family member of a banking dynasty. A fiduciary dictatorship, elected of course, was set in place, one for Asia in Singapore, simply lifted from the Malaysian state, and one for Europe, lifted from France, a mere Duchy, Luxembourg given sovereign and veto power in Europe. In Britain a socialist government, unchallenged, handed the Bank of England over from Parliamentary control. Looking back, where did the first democratic government in Germany come from – the surrender of the state had been unconditional. The country was divided into foreign ruled sectors and Russia had the other half. The country was utterly ruined by city destroying bomber raids and military land operations. Who set it up and who defined the new state's outline? It was certainly not by referendum or mass vote.

Against this shattered culture the universities re-emerged. If the political discourse had turned abstract in Europe, in America the rush to Empire extension left a deeper chaos. The key books referred to with respect and gratitude in this work are nevertheless written in a disintegrating grammatical ethos.

The books without exception are thought in a language already transferred from discourse to summary accountancy. Academic literature, dealing with the exalted subject of social models is as shattered as the bombed cities of Normandy. On the one hand high academic discourse is peppered with the practices of mass-journalism: 'famously' is used on every few pages: sentences begin with prepositions, verbless sentences make headlines: on the other hand nouns are turned into verbs so that nothing can be fixed. 'Foregrounding' becomes an activity. 'Suiciding' becomes something you do, not an event that happened.

Yet the scholars quoted in this work are the last writers touching on the vital issue of our time – the loss of freedom caused by the powerlessness of politics unable to command the world's wealth.

They are the unique restorers of political discourse. They have done it by leading us back, through Marlowe to Seneca and from there to Ovid. The first two, victims of a ruthless political abolition of freedom, and the third banished from Rome to a distant oblivion for speaking the word of freedom – but more than that – re-opening the syntax of a liberated language.

With these heroic writers we arrive at the third level of the power matrix.

10

NOTA BENE II. THE PAST

An overview of the past permits us to see these past events from a symphonic viewpoint, each movement following another.

Christianity. When Rome was in its great power it faced one serious rebellion of slaves. Led by Spartacus, it nearly succeeded until finally defeated by Crassus. This began in 72 BC. When the slave army was broken Crassus made a horrifying example by crucifying some 6,000 of them at regular intervals along the road from Capua to Rome. The mass crucifixion was the warning to all rebels against Rome. The answer of the jewish rebels was brilliant. With a substitute crucified in place of Jesus, Paul was able to make his primal claim – that crucified Jesus had risen from the dead in an act which metaphysicised Spartacus' death into a religion. The crucified man was God become man. He could not save him in this world, but risen, he could save all mankind in the next world. It was what Nietzsche, later, would call a transvaluation of all values. The new slave-based religion triumphed. The Emperor became the Pope. The legion's generals became cardinals. The

Roman language was preserved but its great function – the Senate, was abolished for ever.

After centuries of ruthless control, one which entailed the endless burning of women and heretics by its celibate priesthood, men began to question the price of having lost life responsibility to a divine forgiveness, and thus to begin to reason. Men called it the Enlightenment.

In its fully developed form, thus utterly rejecting the Catholic Rome doctrine of God into man, in its exaltation of reason it swung to an opposite and equal lie. It made man into God. And so, Human Rights acquired capital letters. Man's decree was now absolute because divine.

The new religion had its temple, the Pantheon in Paris. There it buried its high priests. Voltaire's exaltation of reason would deem it be the truth but he could not reasonably explain the Marquis de Sade who dreamed the sexual enslavement of the other, be they male or female. Rousseau's exaltation of the will of the masses would underwrite the vast slaughter of two world wars and two state genocides, Germany's and Russia's.

11

JEAN COCTEAU

"La poésie n'est pas autre chose que le mariage secret du conscient et de l'inconscient. Nous sommes un équilibre entre la conscience et l'inconscience. Et quand nous perdons cet équilibre, nous faisons des sottises, nous sommes alors dans l'inconscience totale.

En somme, qu'est-ce que c'est, par exemple, que les peintures de Dali – ou de Max Ernst – sinon des choses très visibles que les gens reconnaissent tout de suite; des hommes, des montagnes, des déserts et des ombres, de ces hommes sur le sable du déserts… et cependant il y a une énigme dans le tableau, une énigme voulue et visible. Tandis que, par exemple, à l'époque de la Renaissance, les interdictions, les censures religieuses obligeaient les peintres à cacher des choses dans leurs tableaux. Des peintres comme Uccello ou comme Piero

Della Francesca sont des peintres énigmatiques.
Ils arrivaient à glisser ce qu'ils voulaient dire, en
cachette, n'est-ce pas? Aujourd'hui, la cachette est
avouée. C'est le surréalisme. Le surréalisme est
la cachette avouée. C'est dire aux gens: il y a des
secrets, nous allons fouiller ces secrets, nous allons
vivre ces secrets, nous allons vous faire vivre dans
le sommeil."

Jean Cocteau
[Jean Cocteau – 28 Autoportraits
pg. 255. Écriture, 2003]

12

THE OTHER SIDE
OF THE UNDERNEATH

The event, as Laski saw, in its vibrant transformations opened up not merely new situations but also a re-appraisal of ideas, values and the role of each individual in the critical reconstruction of reality that came with each new civic tremor.

As Marlowe had realised below the drama came the re-evaluation and below that came the releasing sublimity of the hidden, mythic forces. Below the drama Marlowe unmasked the epic poem of Lucan, 'The Civil War' and deeper still lay the utterly liberating force of poetry in myth. Ovid, the poet exiled by the world conquerer, Emperor Augustus, to his remote Black Sea dismissal at the limit of the then known end of the world, was able to declare freedom. In writing 'The Metamorphoses' he not only created a directory of his world's myths but he revealed the seething and unstoppable hidden forces that not only had put Augustus in power but as be wrote, were preparing to smash the whole edifice the Emperor had built.

Ted Hughes in 1997 presented his 'Tales from Ovid,' a reading of his key myths, and explained:

'Above all, Ovid was interested in passion … Not just ordinary passion either, but human passion 'in extremis' – passion where it combusts, or levitates, or mutates into an experience of the supernatural.'

In Seneca's greatest play, 'Thyestes' the revenge taken by Atreus on his brother, the macabre feeding up to Thyestes his sons cooked in a feast offered by Atreus is itself a re-enactment of the primal crime of Tantalus serving his son Pelops to feed the gods. Atreus and Thyestes are both sons of Pelops. After the tragedy suffered by Thyestes, which is in Seneca's play, it is in narrative followed by Thyestes taking his revenge through his son Aegisthus who first kills Atreus and then Atreus' son Agamemnon.

So it is that the primal crime of Tantalus stretches forward to the crime of Atreus and beyond that to a generational revenge.

Furia:

Perge, detestabilis umbra, et penates impios furiis age. certetur omni scelere et alterna vice stringatur ensis. nec sit irarum modus pudorve, mentes caecus instiget furor, rabies parentum duret et longum nefas eat in nepotes.

[Seneca: Thyestes: 23-29: Tarrant: American Philological Association]

Forward cursed shade, and drive your sinful house with fury. Make them vie in every kind of crime and draw the sword on either side; let there be no limit to shame in their anger; let a blind fury incite their souls; make the rage of parents last, and make the long trail of sin reach their children's children.

Seneca's 'Thyestes', a drama of father devouring his own children resonates with a conscious echo of Ovid's tale in 'The Metemorphoses'. Tereus takes Procne as his wife. She asks her husband to bring back from Athens her sister, Philomela. Tereus, at the sight of the sister's beauty savagely rapes her. When the two sisters finally meet they are taken with a rage of revenge. Procne murders her own child by Tereus and together the sisters serve him in a feast to the father. In turn the furious father turns on the sisters to kill them. With Ovid, however, another dimension enters human affairs.

> 'Thracius ingenti mensas clamore repellit uipe-
> reasque ciet Stygia de ualle sorores; et modo, si
> posset, reserato pectore diras egerere inde dapes
> semesaque uiscera gestit, flet modo seque uocat
> bustum miserabile nati, nunc sequitur nudo genitas
> Pandione ferro. corpora Cecropidum pennis pen-
> dere putares: pendebant pennis! quarum petit altera
> siluas, altera tecta subit; neque adhuc de pectore
> caedis excessere notae, signataque sanguine pluma
> est. ille dolore suo poenaeque cupidine uelox uerti-
> tur in uolucrem, cui stant in uertice cristae, prominet
> inmodicum praelonga cuspide rostrum. (Nomen
> epops uolucri, facies armata uidetur.)
> [Metamorphoses: V1. 661-674. Ovid:
> Tarrant: Oxford]

Here is Charles Boer's Olson-style rendering. It hints at Ovid's command of psychic states. The end of the savage tale moves from bloody cannibalism to its sublime transformation of the protagonists into beautiful birds of the night.

'The Thracian king shoves table away with great noise, calls snake-sisters from Styx pit! If he could he would cut open his chest and heave the filthy feast of swallowed flesh; he weeps, calls himself son's miserable tomb; sword out, he chases Pandion's daughters: their bodies seem suspended on wings: they are suspended on wings! one, to woods, one under roof: signs of slaughter still not off their breasts, feathers marked with blood; a crested top, unusual beak protruding instead of long sword; his bird name: hoopoe; it has an armed look.'

[Ovid's Metamorphoses: Charles Boer:
Spring Pubs. Texas]

In his 'Tragic Seneca' A.J. Boyle summed up the Senecan ethos:

'The grand machine of the universe, fate, fortune, 'natura', is shown moving through and by means of human psychologies and behaviour in ironic and tragic interaction' – and –

'The patterns of history repeat themselves through and by means of human agents unable to impede their own world's cyclic processes.'
['Tragic Seneca': Boyle 1997. Routledge]

While the Senecan view of a past forcing itself on a tormented present and implying an unfinished affair awaiting the later generation described a closed and in reality doomed view, a tragic view of events and life, it is not the liberating view of our exiled poet at the edge of the world.

With the Ovidian unveiling of the world of myth and arche-
type a new guide is necessary.

The last phase of our recovery of the civic project which itself
is that point where, emerged from the primal jungle and prior to
the collapse back into nature, men and women have lived for a
little in harmony with their children, friends and the animal world,
requires a very special guide.

My guide was the painter, Max Ernst.

Just prior to 1960 I lived in Paris. A Russian friend ran a small
art gallery in the Rue de Rennes. It had two clients, Hans Arp and
Max Ernst. I went to join her most mornings for coffee, one day
there appeared her key artist, Max Ernst. There was an immediate
connection as if already old friends. Then, over a series of long
and intense conversations we surveyed the ruined landscape of
a world irrecoverably desolated by two centuries of war followed
by a hurtling rush into an automated field of numb calm.

Once my painter guide had brushed aside the turbulence of
personalities and ideologies he quickly came to matters he insisted
were the stuff of life.

Max Ernst had been hounded and persecuted by the Nazi
socialist state culminating in his painting 'The Fair Gardener'
being exhibited in the notorious exhibition of 'Decadent Art'
and then being destroyed.

During that decade while Max Ernst was still functioning in
society prior to the totalitarian darkness of the late thirties, D.H.
Lawrence broke from novel and poem to write 'Psycho-analysis
and the Unconscious'.

Lawrence said simply:

> 'We have actually to go back to our own uncon-
> scious. But not to the unconscious which is the

inverted reflection of our ideal consciousness. We must discover, if we can, the true unconscious, where our life bubbles up in us, prior to any mentality. The first bubbling life in us, which is innocent of any mental alteration, this is the unconscious. It is pristine, not in any way ideal. It is the spontaneous origin from which it behooves us to live.'

So it was, one morning in the little gallery on the Rue de Rennes, that the so-named surrealist painter announced to me the judgment of his time:

'You see, Freud had not isolated the Unconscious located in the cortex of a man, what he had done was stumble only half aware on a whole domain. He had discovered anew, the Unseen.'

Beyond the illusion of the scientific observer examining the waking detritus of a dream landscape lay the blurred reality Freud never seemed to face. The great intellect of this remarkable man had found in the forbidding and rejective christian society a niche where he could operate with grudging acceptance, the remote zone of the broken schizophrenic who had failed to function in that society to the point of splitting from it. In his free time he felt more at home with Dostoevsky, Shakespeare, and a smattering of Classic writers. Already could be discerned an intellect that faced two ways. On the one hand the realm of his devastated mental victims and on the other the realm of great writers who envisaged the dilemmas he was still determined to pin down and – not so much cure as render harmless.

In Freud's childhood he recounts how he stood by helpless, while some brute had attacked and insulted his father for being a jew. His forgiveness or rejection of his father may seem to be the Freudian issue of the event, primal to any psycho-analytic process. What concerned Max Ernst – surrealism against science – was why Freud did not submit the father-persecuting thug to his analytical process. He shone no light on the dark chthonic force of bourgeois German culture when it entered its enactments of fantasy, turning a figure that had been Chancellor Hindenburg, and before that Bismarck into the tiny man in the crowd, Adolf Hitler. Instead, silent on the issue, unlike Thomas Mann who fought back however reluctantly, he fled into exile. His most renowned defender Stefan Zweig, too, fled to England only to commit suicide in Brazil.

The event of psycho-analysis in other words had been destroyed by the breaking of the window which had permitted its view into the hidden world of the Unconscious. Laing had made the correct diagnosis – madness was not uniquely embedded in the brain of the patient but rather in the societal nexus. In the compulsive act of destroying psycho-analysis, and of course, its creator, he turned away from the malady, man in society.

Lionel Trilling regretfully observed Laing's failure to stay on target. Those who identified society as the invalid all settled for a sociological structuring thus plunging the post-freudian world into a fated support of a planned society which disastrously licenced its offspring, the planned economy.

Max Ernst's vision united the various worlds of experience but saw them emerging from and manifest by and disappearing with man the in-time creature on the threshold of invisible realities.

It was not a cultural chance but a cultural necessity which determined that the narrative of human conflict be seen anew by painters and sculptors. Max Ernst, Hans Arp, de Chirico, Dali, were men who could describe a world rather than recount a crime.

Max Ernst saw existence as a unified field that bound together the historic event, the lived out passions and the natural world of growth, production and decay. In the same way he recognised that the human reality, emergent from nature, brought with it ancient patterns of selfhood, conflict and locked unresolved forces.

The passions try to force the present to be an arena of revenge, finally working out the ancient crime at the same time as the awakened self tries to construct a fresh and future reality.

Man was a creature from wild nature, both destroyer and maker of the new. Poised between a vanished half-remembered past and a part-achieved and still not manifest future.

In 1937 his painting, 'The Fair Gardener' was exhibited as decadent art by the Nazi regime and destroyed. In 1967 he created a painting entitled 'The Return of the Fair Gardener.' The sublime manifest in the paintings of Ernst as it did in the poetry of Marlowe and the myths recounted by Ovid.

With the event called history, and all passion spent, and with worlds crumbling into ruin and tangled undergrowth over forgotten tombs, the words remain – the witness, the evidence, the proof of luminosity and life.

Ovid ends his 'Metamorphoses' thus:

> 'Iamque opus exegi, quod nes Iouis ira nec ignis nec poterit ferrum nec edax abolere uetustas. cum dulet, illa dies, quae nil nisi corporis huius ius habet, incerti spatium mihi finiat aeui; parte tamen meliore mei super alta perennis astra ferar, nomenque erit indelebile nostrum; quaque patet domitis Romana potentia terris ore legar populi, perque omnia saecula fama(si quid habent ueri uatum praesagia) uiuam.

[Ovidi: Metamorphoses:
15. 871-879. Tarrant. Oxford]

'And now I've finished the work: and not Jove-wrath, fire, sword, or time-bite can destroy it; when it so pleases that day with power over nothing but my body, my uncertain life-span ends: but with my better part I'll be borne above the stars forever, and my name will be indelible: wherever Roman power reaches, conquered lands, I'll be read: and with fame through all ages, if poets' predictions are true at all, I'll live.

[Ovid's Metamorphoses:
trans. Charles Boer. Spring Pubs]

13

POSTSCRIPT

In this proposed model of the human situation everything and everyone is in motion. The times move in a natural cycle from primitive tribe to kingship, aristocracy to mass rule and inevitably re-formed to dictatorship and so on. At the same time, or rather, in the same process man in the mass sees a man emerge, a like group surround him, until corrupted, turn in on themselves prompting the mass to rise up and cleanse the time. Different times mean different mores mean different men.

Since we cannot choose which zone is to be preferred or even which kind of man really we should be, fated to a particular time and a particular parenthood we then must fulfil or go beyond the given lived moment of the cycle.

It is that circle of men and women bounded not by blood or station, but by a shared quality of life which demands pure worship of the Lord of the Universe, an on-going competition among its members in generosity, support, nurture, learning and mutual concern.

Ibn Khaldun said that such a circle would always triumph over its enemies but added that if such a group were bonded in worship of the Divine they would have the great triumph.

Ibn Khaldun states:

> The science of the interpretation of dreams is a part of the religious sciences…whatever it is the dream is common to the whole human species without exception and it must be interpreted.

In the Noble Qur'an it relates in the Sura-Yusuf:

> "'O counsellors! Explain my dream to me if you are those who can interpret visions!' They said, 'A jumbled mass of mixed-up dreams! We do not know the meaning of such things.' The one of them who had been saved (Yusuf) then said, remembering after a period, 'I will tell you what it signifies, so send me out.'
> [Noble Qur'an: 12. 43-45. Bewley]

Ibn Khaldun:

> "It is established in the 'Sahih' coming from the Messenger and Abu Bakr, 'The dream belongs to perceptions of the Unseen…' after finishing the Dawn Prayer the Messenger would question his Companions: 'Did anyone of you see in a dream last night?' He asked that to benefit from its warnings or good signals."
> [Le Livre des Examples: Pleiade: Vol 1. 956]

Ibn Khaldun indicates that binding factor which unites a brotherhood, in itself a spiritual bond, as being 'asabiyya', while it translates as 'esprit de corps' it is both subtler and stronger. The emergent atheist and rationalist movement of the Enlightenment tried to revive it as a child of Revolution reducing it to a structural, ritualistic and outwardly initiate circle naming them freemasons to hint at an ancient origin. Nothing is further from its character.

This inner circle of human society is not the law of the land, but it does not overthrow the law. Society has its structures and needs its leaders, and as we have established they may at one point raise up a leader and at another a ruling group and at another the forms may collapse. However, the governance of society where it is the responsibility of a man in his time, at the same time a man must live to the best of his knowledge. The lived life must be self directed not dependent on the whim of epoch. The lived life is dependent on the company of a few. Divine Messengers confirmed or revised societal law but they drew their strength from a chosen circle of quality. Jesus's followers were gathered at a divinely given table to feast their brotherhood. The final Messenger names ten men as assured the Garden in the Unseen, they were the chosen and the best of men.

* * * * *

Qur'an opens with the key guidance of the final means:

> "Alif Lam Mim
> That is the Book, without any doubt.
> It contains guidance for those who have Taqwa (awe
> of god): those who have trust in the Unseen and

establish salat and give of what We have provided
for them"

Under this final dispensation of knowledge we should live with
a great expectation in life made all the more luminous as the age
increases in darkness. It will not be possible alone. Essential are
a few Companions for company in the dark.

THE END

14

APPENDIX

An excerpt from the Qur'anic Tafsir and Ishara of Shaykh Ahmad ibn 'Ajiba, the greatest of the sufic scholars. Translation by Shaykh Habib Bewley.

———

Shaykh Ibn Ajiba, may Allah have mercy on him, says:

> Allah says,
> **"Perhaps you may destroy yourself with grief, chasing after them, if they do not have iman in these words. We made everything on the earth adornment for it so that we could test them to see whose actions are the best. We will certainly make everything on it a barren wasteland." [Al-Kahf: 6-8]**

The Haqq says, **"Perhaps,"** O Muhammad, **"you may destroy yourself"** and kill yourself with your sorrow and distress at the fact that your people are holding back from becoming believers and parting ways with you, **"chasing after them"** when they turn away from you as you call them to Allah. Because of how upset he felt when they turned away, Allah compares him to one whose loved ones depart, leaving him standing in their footprints, grief-stricken and destroying himself because of the strong sense of sorrow that has taken hold of him, **"if they do not have iman in these words"** i.e. in the Qur'an, which Allah refers to in the beginning of this *sura* as the Book. You did all this out of **"grief"** i.e. your extreme sorrow and regret about them.

Then Allah gives the reason for their turning away from belief, namely, their being deluded and dazzled by the adornment of this world. He says, **"We made everything on the earth"**, its trees, flowers and fruits, its minerals and precious metals, all that can be worn or eaten, all that can be ridden or married, **"adornment for it"** splendid and delightful, bringing enjoyment to those who see it. They benefit from it in terms of what they eat and wear, and in terms of what they see and learn, for even snakes and scorpions have their use and serve their purpose, helping to remind us of the punishment of the Hereafter. Indeed, every event that takes place in this world is a form of adornment, since they all indicate the Creator. And the same applies to wives and children, and indeed they are among the greatest of its adornments. All of these things are a trial, which We made **"so that we could test them"**, try them until it becomes clear **"whose actions are the best"** which of them has *zuhd* in it, and moves towards Allah with right action, for there is no action better than *zuhd* in this world, since it is the reason that one dedicates his time to various forms of worship, whether they relate to the body or to the heart.

Abu as-Saʻud said, "The best of actions is having *zuhd* in this world and not being overly concerned about it; being satisfied with a little and spending out from it on what matters; reflecting on where it comes from and using it as a means to increase in knowledge of its Creator; deriving enjoyment of it to the degree that the Law permits and fulfilling its rights; being thankful for its blessings and careful not to use them for corrupt ends or as a means to give free rein to the appetites, as the unbelievers and the people of whim do.

"We will certainly make everything on it" when this world comes to its end **"a barren wasteland"** i.e. arid earth without any plant life, after it had been land whose magnificence astonished the gaze and made people feel privileged to have seen it with their own eyes. Only those who have no intellect are deceived by that which fades away and does not last, so do not be surprised that they turn away - they have no intellects.

It is probable that this was revealed to console the Prophet, may Allah bless him and grant him peace, for it guides him to see the plan of the Haqq, putting his heart at ease about their having rejected him, since he is withdrawn from forms in the company of the Former, the Planner, and withdrawn from adornment in the company of the Adorner. Creation is but a manifestation and reflection of the Attributes, and he was withdrawn into the Essence, which is their source, by the annihilation of the outward and annihilation of the actions, as He clearly indicates with His Words, **"We will certainly make…."**

Ishara: Elite-hood, looking at it for what it actually is, has a beginning and an end. Part of the state of the people of the beginning is the strength of their desire for good, both for themselves and for the rest of the slaves of Allah. They wish for all people to be right-acting and part of the elite, and so when they see people turn away, they feel great sorrow on their behalf, and when they see people come forward, they feel great joy on their behalf, because more of the slaves of Allah have been guided.

Then, when they gain a strong foothold and become firmly established in the ranks of the elite and undergo the greater annihilation, they no longer feel that strong desire, and so feel no sorrow when they, or anyone else, misses out. So this reproach for the strong desire they feel in the beginning may be directed their way in order to help complete them and enable them to rise to the perfected station.

Allah's Words, **"We made everything on the earth…"** are the reason why many people remain outside of the elite, and set apart those who seek from those who turn away. Those who are drawn in by the adornment and splendour of this world miss out on the rank of elite-hood and remain among the ranks of the common people, while those who turn away from this world and its magnificence and turn with their heart to Allah, join the ranks of the elite and are brought close to Allah.

This, then, is the best of actions, by means of which Allah tests His slaves, and which is referred to in His Words, **"so that we could test them to see whose actions are the best."** In a hadith, we find, "This world is the wealth of those who have no wealth. It is hoarded by those who have no intellect, and fought over by those who have no knowledge." There are a great many hadiths relating to zuhd and desire and they have been the subject of many a book. All success comes from Allah.

Then He starts to relate the story of the people of the Cave, saying,

> **"Do you consider that the Companions of the Cave and Ar-Raqim were one of the most remarkable of Our Signs? When the young men took refuge in the cave and said, 'Our Lord, give us mercy directly from You and open the**

**way to right guidance for us in our situation.'
So We sealed their ears with sleep in the cave
for a number of years. Then We woke them up
again so that we might see which of the two
groups would better calculate the time they had
stayed there." [Al-Kahf: 9-12]**

The Haqq says, **"Do you consider"** i.e. 'Have you thought, O
Muhammad', although what is meant here is whether his *umma*
have considered **"that the Companions of the Cave"** a *kahf* is
a broad cave in a mountain. As for its exact location, there is a
difference of opinion - some say it is near Palestine, and some
say it is in al-Andalus near Loja in the province of Granada. Ibn
Atiya mentions that he went into their cave and found dead bodies
there accompanied by a dog, and a mosque built over them. And
nearby, there was a building called ar-Raqim, the foundation of
whose walls remained in place. And in that province, there are
ruins called 'the city of Diqyus'. Allah knows best.

> Ibn Juzayy said, "One of the things that make this
> unlikely is that it has been narrated that Muaw-
> iya passed by their cave and wanted to go inside,
> but refrained from doing so out of reverence and
> respect, and it is known that Muawiya never went
> near al-Andalus. Another is that the dead bodies of
> Loja were visible to all and no one experienced the
> fear and dread that Allah mentions with respect to
> the people of the Cave."

The well-known position is that ar-Raqim is the tablet upon which
their names and lineage were written, and which was placed by

the king in his treasury. This tablet was made out of either lead or stone, and he had commanded that their names be written on it when their families had come to him complaining that they had gone missing. Ar-Raqim is also said to be the name of their dog.

That is to say, 'Did you think that they, **"were"**, i.e. their story was, **"one of"** i.e. ranked amongst **"the most remarkable of Our Signs?"** i.e. that it was something wondrous unlike the rest of Our Signs. Such is not the case. What this means is that even though their story was miraculous in nature, it is not really remarkable when compared with Allah's other Signs, most remarkable of which is His creation of uncountable types and species from a single substance. Compared to that what happened to them is the most trivial and insignificant of things. Al-Qushayri said, "He removed whatever wonder and disbelief might be felt towards their story by linking their affair to Himself, and declaring that they are part of **"Our Signs"**, for it cannot be denied nor thought contrived that Allah is capable of turning the norms of existence on their head."

Then He mentions the beginning of their story, saying, **"When the young men took refuge"** *fitya* is the plural of *fata*, which means a young man who is in the fullness of his youth. In other words, 'Remember when the young men took refuge in the cave, fleeing on account of their deen, afraid for their faith on account of the unbelievers, led by Daqyanus, as will be mentioned later in their story. " They **"said"** when they entered into the cave, **"'Our Lord, give us…directly from You"** from the innermost workings of Your affair and from Your special treasure trove of mercy that is kept hidden and out of view of all that is normal and day-to-day, **"…mercy…"** a special form of mercy bringing us ease and comfort and keeping us safe from our enemies, **"and open the way…"** make things right **"…for us in our situation"** the path we have taken to cut ourselves off from the unbelievers and leave them behind, **"...to right guidance..."** guidance by means of which we can become rightly guided. Or it could mean, 'Make our entire affair one of right guidance.' Short grammatical discussion. Or it could mean, 'Enable us to find the path that leads to what is sought.' The root meaning of *tahyi'a* is creating a thing's outward form.

"So We sealed their ears with sleep" i.e. We made them sleep. To indicate the sort of deep sleep that allows no sound to enter the ears, Allah uses the metaphor of a seal and a block being placed upon them. Despite the fact that all the other senses are also blocked during sleep, Allah singles out the ears for mention because the seal and block is greater than the others, since it is by means of them that people are usually woken up. The *fa* in *fa-darabna* is like the *fa* in *fa-stajabna lahu* after Allah words *idh naadaa* [al-Anbiya: 9]. Thus, the aforementioned sealing of their ears, the sun being kept to the left of them and to the right, and their being woken up, all of this was a gift to them of pure direct mercy, kept hidden and out of view of those who cling to the day-to-day means of existence, and was in answer to their supplication. In other words, we responded to their supplication and put them to sleep **"in the cave for a number of years"** i.e. years that were made up of a number of them, or years that may be counted and assigned a number. The reasons the years are described in this way may be because there were so many of them, which would be most appropriate if we consider the Power of Allah, or because there were so few, which would be most appropriate if we consider the fact that Allah rejects the fact of this story being anything particularly remarkable when compared to His other wondrous Signs - with Allah, the length of time they remained there is no different to a small portion of one day.

"**Then We woke them up again**" i.e. woke them from their deathlike slumber "**so that we might see**" know through seeing, i.e. so that our Knowledge could have a connection in the present like its primary connection which was a connection to what was yet to be, "**which of the two groups**" which of the positions of the two different groups regarding how long they had spent there, which is referred to later in Allah's Words, "'We have been here for a day...'", "**would better calculate**" i.e. were more precise in their calculations concerning how long "**...they had stayed there**" i.e. the length of their stay there in terms of "**time...**" i.e. the full extent of it. This demonstrates to them and others their incapacity and makes them more fully hand their affair over to the All-Knowing, All-Aware. It heightens their awareness of their own circumstances and what Allah has done for them, in terms of preserving their bodies and their deen, and increases them in the certainty of their belief in the completeness of His Knowledge and Power. It gives them complete certainty as to the truth of the Resurrection. This was as a mercy and kindness to the believers of their time, a clear proof against the unbelievers, and a lesson to those who were yet to come. This is all part of the wisdom of their being woken up again after having being put asleep. Allah is the All-Knowing, All-Wise.

Ishara: If someone cuts himself off and turns to Allah completely, and takes refuge in the cave of His care, and places no hope whatsoever in the kindness of created beings, it is Allah's wont to watch over him with the eye of His solicitude and concern, and keep him safe under his care. Then when he becomes ensconced in the protective sanctuary of His mercy, and shaded under the expansive shadow of His right guidance, He will prevent his heart from hearing the sounds of what will muddy and distract it, and his eyes from seeing other than Him. All success is from Allah.

Then He relates their story in full, saying:

> **"We will relate their story to you with truth. They were young men who had iman in their Lord and We increased them in guidance. We fortified their hearts when they stood up and said, 'Our Lord is the Lord of the heavens and the earth and We will not call on any god apart from Him. We would in that case have uttered an abomination. These people of ours have taken gods apart from Him. Why do they not produce a clear authority concerning them? Who could do greater wrong than someone who invents a lie against Allah? When you have separated yourselves from them and everything they worship except Allah, take refuge in the cave and your Lord will unfold His mercy to you and open the way to the best for you in your situation.'"** [Al-Kahf: 13-16]

The Haqq says, **"We will relate their story to you"** a *naba'* is an account of something that is weighty and carries importance, we will relate a story **"with truth"** true words unsullied by falsehood or doubt.

Their story, according to Muhammad ibn Ishaq, is that the people of the Injil had fallen into disarray, with mistaken beliefs becoming commonplace among them. Their rulers had exceeded their bounds and started to worship idols and make sacrifices to false gods. One of the worst among them, a king who was guilty of the worst excesses and was unparalleled in his insolence, was Daqyanus. He far exceeded the bounds, and ransacked people's lands and houses, rampaging right through them and spreading corruption in his wake. He took it upon himself to kill all his opponents who clung to the religion of the *Masih*. He would pursue them and when he caught them, he would give them a choice, "Die, or worship idols." Those who desired this lower world followed him and did as he did, while those who preferred the abode of everlasting life were maimed and killed, and then hung up from the city walls and on the city gates. When these young men, each of whom was a prince and one of the leading men of the city, when they saw this happening, they began earnestly to entreat their Lord and fill their times with prayer and supplication. While they were thus engaged, the tyrant's men came upon them and brought them into his presence, whereupon he addressed them and gave them the choice between death or worshipping idols. They replied, "We have a god whose power and greatness fill the heavens and earth. We will never call on any one else apart from Him, and we will never agree to do what you have called us to do, so do what you must." So he commanded that their fine clothing be torn from their backs and that they be removed from his presence. In one narration, it relates that their families then came forward and spoke up on their behalf. Then the tyrant left to go to the city of Nineveh to conduct some business, but before he went, he told them they should use the time he was away to reflect on their situation, and consider their choice carefully. 'If you do not do as I ask,' he told them, 'I will do to you what I have done to the rest of the believers.'

So the young men decided to flee and take refuge in the fortified and inaccessible cave. Each of them took something from the homes of his parents and gave some of it away as *sadaqa* and packed the rest for their trip. Then they took refuge in the cave. In one narration, it states that they passed by the dog on their way and it followed them. Its part in the story will be mentioned in due course. In the cave, they spent their entire time, morning and night, praying and making fervent supplications to their Lord. As for their day-to-day dietary needs, they appointed one of their number, Yamlikha, to oversee them and take care of them. Every morning, he would remove his fine clothes and don instead the clothes of the poor. Then he would go into the city where he would buy them provisions and find out what news there was regarding their position with the king. They continued in this way until the tyrant returned to the city and sought them out, summoning their parents into his presence. But they spoke out in their own defense saying that their sons had disobeyed them and stolen their money, squandering it in the market-place, and had then fled to the mountains.

When Yamlikha saw these terrible developments unfold, he returned to his companions weeping, bringing with him only a small amount of provision. He told them about the horrors he had witnessed, and in their fear they turned to Allah and fell down in prostration before him. Then they sat up and started to discuss among themselves the implications of their situation, and it was while they were sitting thus that Allah sealed their ears, and they fell asleep on the spot with their provisions lying beside their heads.

Daqyanus marched out from the city with all his horses and all his men to search for them, and found out that they had entered the cave. So he commanded his men to bring them out, but not one of them was able to step inside. When they had exhausted every avenue in their attempts and realised their incapacity, one of them said to the tyrant, "Is it not so that were you to lay hands on them, you would simply kill them?" He replied, "Yes, that is so. Build a gate to block the entrance to the cave and leave them inside to starve to death." So they did as he commanded.

As for who those young men were, Allah describes them, saying, **"They were young men"** In grammatical terms, this is the start of a completely new sentence. It is as if someone asked a question about the state of these young man, and Allah responded with these words: they were young men in the full bloom of youth **"who had iman in their Lord"** by using the word *rabb* - Lord, Allah turns our attention to His Attribute of Lordship, the quality which kept them protected and sustained, **"and We increased them in guidance"** by giving them the strength and resolve to endure what they were forced to endure, and acquainting them with some of our most hidden blessings by which they came to prefer annihilation over remaining. In this *aya*, Allah changes from the third person to the first person to indicate the increase in His care and concern for them. **"We fortified their hearts"** i.e. We strengthened them and gave them the fortitude to bear being forsaken by their families and separated from their homes, their brothers and their possessions. We emboldened them to openly speak the truth without caution or fear, and to reply to the tyrant, Daqyanus **"when they stood up"** i.e. when they stood bolt upright in defense of their deen. Mujahid said, "They left the city and came upon one another without having made an appointment to meet. Then the eldest amongst them said, 'I have come to a realisation within myself. My Lord is the Lord of the heavens and the earth.' They replied, 'We are like you.' So they all stood up together **"and said, 'Our Lord is the Lord of the heavens and the earth,"** and resolved to hold firm and not waver in making that affirmation. It is also said that they stood up in the presence of the tyrant as he took them to task for abandoning the worship of idols without feeling the slightest degree of concern for what he had to say. If that is the case, then Allah's Words in the beginning of the next aya, **"These people..."** must be considered as separate from the words that precede them, since they were said after they had left the presence of the tyrant.

Then they said, **"and We will not call on any god apart from Him"** not independent of Him nor in partnership with Him. The reason they used the word *ilaah* - 'god' and not the word *rabb* - 'lord' was to refute the claims of their opponents that their idols were 'gods'. It was also to let them know that it is upon the quality of *uluhiyya* that *'ubudiyya* is centred. **"We would in that case have uttered an abomination"** words that go beyond the proper bounds. In other words, 'We would have committed an outrage and been excessive in our unbelief, we would have said something unconscionable and irrational, were we to have called on something other than Allah, believing that thing to be a god.

"These people of ours have taken gods apart from Him" the construction of this sentence indicates their denial of what their people have done. **"Why do they not produce...concerning them"** i.e. concerning their being gods, **"...a clear authority...?"** i.e. incontestable proof. **"Who could do greater wrong"** i.e. there is no one who does greater wrong **"than someone who invents a lie against Allah"** by associating a partner to Him. Such a person is guilty of greater wrongdoing than every wrongdoer.

"When you have separated yourselves from them" i.e. cut yourselves off from their company **"and"** separated yourselves from **"everything they worship except Allah, take refuge in the cave"** In other words, 'after you have separated yourselves from them at the level of belief, separate yourselves from them at a physical level", **"and your Lord will unfold...to you"** will liberally bestow upon you **"...His Mercy..."** in both this abode and the Next, **"and open the way...for you in your situation'"** the situation in which you currently find yourselves of fleeing on account of your deen, **"...to the best..."** that which brings you profit and gain. The purity of their certainty regarding this and the strength of their confidence was all by the favour of Allah, and Allah knows best.

Ishara: In Allah's description of the people of the Cave, he mentions five qualities, each of which is a defining feature of the *Sufiyya*: *Iman* - 'belief', which is the foundation; increasing in right guidance by developing the certainty to arrive at a pure *'irfan*; tying the heart to the presence of the Lord; standing up to make the truth manifest, or on account of being overcome by extreme ecstasy or passion; and expressing the truth without caring what any created being thinks.

Al-Wartajabi said regarding Allah's Words, **"and We increased them in guidance"**, "i.e. We increased them in light from Our Beauty, and they were guided by it along the paths of knowledge of My Essence and My Attributes. And that light will continue to increase them in clarity forever, since there is no end to My light." Then he said about Allah's Words, **"when they stood up"**, "Some of the shuyukh have taken this *aya* as proof for the movements made by those overcome with ecstasy during the *dhikr*, for when hearts are connected to the *malakut*, to the place of Absolute Purity, they are moved by the different forms of *dhikr* and types of *sama'*. The root of this is Allah's Words, **"We fortified their hearts when they stood up"**. Yes, this meaning only applies if the standing that is referred to is actual bodily function, a physical standing. However, if the word *qiyam* comes in the context of care and protection, and the word *rabt* in the context of being transported from a place of inconstancy to a place of solidity and establishment, then taking it as proof of being still and motionless in the midst of ecstasy would be better, since *rabt* can have the meaning of making still and *qiyam* the meaning of going straight."

I say, "The upshot of this is that if we understand standing at a physical level, the *aya* proves to the people of the beginning that standing in the nights of *dhikr* is permissible; and if we understand it at a metaphysical level, i.e that it refers to something rising up or going straight, then there is proof in it for the people of the end that they should be still and not move. It is as if it alludes to the story of Junayd in terms of his beginning and his end, and Allah knows best.

Ibn Lubb said, "The difference of opinion amongst the *'ulama* with respect to standing to do *dhikr* of Allah is well known, but the *Sufiyya* consider it permissible and have done it and continue to do it, inferring its permissibility from Allah's Words concerning the people of the cave, **"when they stood up and said, 'Our Lord is the Lord of the heavens and the earth"**, even if the aya can be understood in a different light."

I say, "Allah's Words, **"Those who do dhikr of Allah standing and sitting" [Ali Imran: 191]** unambiguously declares it to be permissible."

He says in al-Qut, "We have narrated that he, may Allah bless him and grant him peace, passed by a man who was sighing out loud and exhibiting signs of ecstasy and rapture. One of the men who was with him said, 'Messenger of Allah, do you see what he is doing as showing off?' The Prophet, may Allah bless him and grant him peace, replied, 'No, rather he is soft-hearted and penitent.' And he said of another, 'Does he raise his voice when reciting the aya! Recite so Allah can hear you, not so that you can be heard by others!', thereby disapproving of what he saw in him. But he did not disapprove of Abu Musa when he said, 'If I had known that you could hear me, I would have made my recitation more beautiful for you,' since his intention in that was good. So if someone does an act openly with good intention, such an action cannot be considered to be showing off, since it is free of any worldly impulses. It is not done in the desire for praise and craving for recognition."

Then He mentions their state in the cave, saying,

> **"You would have seen the sun, when it rose, inclining away from their cave towards the right, and, when it set, leaving them behind on the left, while they were lying in an open part of it. That was one of Allah's Signs. Whoever Allah guides is truly guided. But if He misguides someone, you will find no protector for them to guide them rightly. You would have supposed them to be awake whereas in fact they were asleep. We moved them to the right and to the left, and, at the entrance, their dog stretched out its paws. If you had looked down and seen them, you would have turned from them and run and have been filled with terror at the sight of them." [Al-Kahf: 17-18]**

The Haqq says, shedding light on their state and situation after they had taken refugee in the cave, **"You would have seen the sun, when it rose, inclining"** i.e. leaning **"away from their cave"** i.e. the cave in which they had taken refuge. The one who is being addressed by this aya is either the Messenger of Allah, may Allah bless him and grant him peace,, or each and every person who meets the preconditions for being addressed. But Allah is not saying that he, may Allah bless him and grant him peace, actually saw or will see it with his naked eye, but rather that were he to have been in a position where he could see it, he would have seen the sun, when it rose, inclining away from their cave **"towards the right"**, i.e. in the direction of the side of the cave which is to the right of you as you enter it, **"and, when it set,"** i.e. and you would have seen it when it set **"leaving them behind"** i.e. being cut off from them and going past them **"on the left,"** i.e. in the direction of the side of it which is adjacent to the west. This was accomplished by Allah causing the sun to move in an extraordinary and abnormal way, a miracle given by Him to the people of the cave. It has also been said that the entrance to the cave faced westward in the direction of Ursa Major. **"while they were lying in an open part of it"** in a wide-open section of it, an area upon which the sun would normally shine, but upon which it did not in the case of the people of the cave because Allah had kept it away from them.

"That was one of Allah's Signs" i.e. what Allah did for them with respect to His causing the sun to incline away from them as it rose and as it set was one of His signs that indicate the perfection of His knowledge and power, the excellence of *tawhid* and the degree to which Allah honours His people. One of the *'ulama* said, "This was before Daqyanus blocked the entrance to the cave." I say, "This was both before it was blocked and after the blockage was destroyed, since it was destroyed at a later date. For when the people of the cave awoke, they found the way out of the cave open and the blockage destroyed." A literal reading of the aya supports the position that something miraculous took place.

"Whoever Allah guides is truly guided" and obtains success. This is meant either to praise them, bear witness to the fact that they had done what was required of them, and tell that they had realised their hopes of His mercy being showered upon them; or to alert us to the fact that Signs of this sort are numerous, but the only ones who gain from them are those whom Allah guides and to whom He grants success. **"But if He misguides someone,"** i.e. if He creates misguidance in him by turning his choice in its direction, **"you will find...for them"** even if you exhaust every avenue in your search, **"... no protector ..."** no backer **"to guide them rightly"** to guide them to the success that is mentioned. This sentence is a parenthesis, inserted within the main body of the story.

Then He says, **"You would have supposed them"** thought them **"to be awake"** either because of the fact that their eyes were open or because of how much they were moving back and forth. **"Whereas in fact they were asleep. We moved them"** while they were sleeping **"to the right"** i.e. over onto their righthand sides, **"and to the left"** i.e. over on to their lefthand sides, so that the earth would not eat away at the parts of their bodies that were in contact with the ground. Ibn Abbas said, "If they had not moved about, the earth would have consumed them." Some say they moved twice in the course of each year, others that they moved once on the Day of Ashura, and others that they moved once every nine years.

"and...their dog stretched out its paws". The *dhiraa'* is the section of the arm that stretches from the elbow to the tips of the finger, **"...at the entrance..."** over a spot within the cave, or by the open area just inside the cave, or on the threshold. It is said that this was a dog they passed by on their way to the cave and it started to follow them. They tried again and again to chase it away so that it would stop coming back. So Allah gave it the power of speech and it said to them, "Friends of Allah, do not fear that I will be the source of any harm or affliction for you. I am but a creature who loves the lovers of Allah. So go to sleep and I will keep watch for you." It is also said that it was the dog of a shepherd they encountered upon the way. This shepherd followed them in their deen and went with them, and his dog came too. This interpretation is strengthened by the alternative reading, "and their *kaalib* stretched out" A *kaalib* is one who owns a dog. It is also said that it was a hunting dog that belonged to them. As for its colour, there is a difference of opinion - some say that it was red, some say yellow, and some say light-brown.

"If you had looked down and seen them," i.e. if you were to have seen them with your own eyes. *ittilaa'* is looking down at something from above, **"you would have turned from them and run"** you would have fled at the sight of them **"and have been filled with terror at the sight of them."** i.e. fear would have filled your heart at the terrifying spectacle, and that is either because Allah clad them in a terrifying cloak of fear, or because of how huge their bodies were and how wide open their eyes. For their eyes were open in the manner of someone who is wide awake and about to say something. It has been narrated that when Muawiyya invaded Byzantium, he passed by the cave and said, "Would that the way be opened for us to these young men so that we can look upon them." Ibn Abbas replied, "You will not be able to. Allah has prevented one better than yourself from doing it, when He addressed the Prophet saying, **"If you had looked down and seen them…""** But Muawiyya would not listen and said, "I will not stop until I have learnt something definitive about them." So he sent people to the cave, saying, ""Go and look," and they did as he commanded. But when they entered the cave, Allah sent a wind that set them on fire.

Ishara: There is a strong resemblance between the *Sufiyya* and the people of the cave in terms of how they devote themselves to

Allah and rid themselves of everything other than Him; how they enter into His enclosure and flee from everything that distracts them from Him; and how they seek out direct mercy from Allah and ask that He open the way for them to every form of guidance and right action. It was for this reason that the Shaykh and Qutb, Ibn Mashish, concluded his famous *as-Salaat al-Mashishiya* with the supplication made by them when they took refuge in the cave of refuge, drawing a comparison between them and the people of *tariqa* with respect to the totality of their withdrawal and flight from the zone of the sensory. And because of how closely their situation resembles that of the people of the cave, Allah has undertaken to protect the *Sufiyya* from those who wish them harm, caused them to withdraw from their sensory selves, and made them witness to the wonders of His *lutf* and power. So complete is this resemblance that you seldom find a group of them travelling without there being a dog following them and attaching itself to their group. Indeed, I myself bore witness to this on the majority of the journeys I undertook in the company of the *fuqara*, confirming how complete and precise the likeness is. And Allah knows best.

Then He mentions their being awoken from their sleep, saying:

> **"That was the situation when we woke them up so they could question one another. One of them asked, 'How long have you been here?' They replied, 'We have been here for a day or part of a day.' They said, 'Your Lord knows best how long you have been here. Send one of your number into the city with this silver you have, so he can see which food is purest and bring you some of it to eat. But he should go about**

with caution so that no one is aware of you, for if they find out about you they will stone you or make you revert to their religion and then you will never have success.'" [Al-Kahf: 19-20]

The Haqq says, **"That was the situation when"** i.e. in the same way that We put them to sleep and protected their bodies from affliction and decomposition, something which was in itself a sign of the perfection of Our power, **"we woke them up"** we awoke them from their slumber **"so they could question one another"** either so they could hear the consummate wisdom that would be uttered as a result, or so that they could gain understanding of their situation and knowledge of what their Lord had done to them, and through that, obtain even greater certainty as to the perfection of the Power of Allah and first-hand knowledge of the manner of the resurrection, and express their gratitude and thanks for the blessings Allah had bestowed upon them.

"One of them asked" The one who asked this was their chief, whose name was Mixelmina, **"'How long have you been here?'"** i.e 'How long have you been sleeping?' It is possible that he asked this because of how much they had changed, as normally happens when a large amount of time passes. **"They replied,"** i.e. some of them replied, **"'We have been here for a day or part of a day,'"** It is said that they answered in this way because they had entered the cave in the morning and when they awoke, it was evening. The first thing they said when they awoke was, **"'We have been here for a day"** But when they saw that the sun had still not set, they said, **"or part of a day,'"** They were merely saying what they believed to be most likely, and so this cannot be considered to be a lie on their part.

"**They said**" i.e. others among them said when they noticed signs on them that indicated a longer time had passed, such as the fact that their nails and hair had become very long, "**'Your Lord knows best how long you have been here**" i.e. 'You have no idea how long you have been here, only Allah knows.' This reply of theirs to those who had spoken first was made in the most courteous way possible, "**Send one of your number into the city with this silver you have,**" They set aside their discussion of how much time had passed and moved on to the matter that was far more pressing for them at that particular time. The word *wariq* is a synonym for *fidda* - silver, regardless of whether that silver has been minted into coins or not. The fact that the word 'this' is used to describe it shows that it refers to a specific piece of silver that was to be used to buy them provisions for that day. The fact that they had this silver in their possession proves that there is no contradiction between having reliance on Allah and packing provisions for the way. Indeed, our Prophet , may Allah bless him and grant him peace, himself used to take provisions with him when he went up to the cave of Hira to devote himself to the worship of his Lord. Then they said, "**so he can see which**" i.e. which of its inhabitants has the "**food**" which "**is purest**" i.e. most *halal* and wholesome, or most plentiful and cheap, "**and bring you some of it to eat**" i.e. some of that food which is most pure. "**But he should go about with caution**" i.e. you must be discreet when you enter the city and buy the food, "**so that**" no one recognises you and "**no one is**" made "**aware of you,**" i.e. so that no one can tell anyone who you are or that you are in the city. Or it means that you should be careful not to do anything to draw attention to yourself and cause that to happen.

Then they give the reason why no one should be made aware of him, saying, "**for if they find out about you**" if they discover you or lay hands upon you. The pronoun, 'they' refers back to the people of the city. In other words, if the people of the city get hold of you, **"they will stone you"** if you continue to hold firm to this path you have chosen **"or make you revert to their religion"** i.e. they will make you come back to it and force you to become part of it again, much like Allah's Words elsewhere in the Qur'an: "unless you return to our religion" [Ibrahim: 16]. It is said that originally they were upon the religion of the people of their city and then they went against them when they saw the Truth. **"and then you will not have success'"** if you do revert to it, even if you have done so under duress, **"ever"**, not in this world and not in the Next. This is about as clear-cut a warning as you could get.

Ishara: In the same way, we have woken up those who turn towards us from the sleep of heedlessness and ignorance so that they can question one another and come to recognise the extent to which Allah has blessed them by granting them wakefulness and by saving them from idleness and inactivity. When they wake up from the sleep of heedlessness, they see the insignificance and valuelessness of those days of idleness, since days of heedlessness have little weight even when they stretch out for a very long period of time. It says in the Hikam, "A life may encompass a vast expanse of time, but weigh very little." The time of wakefulness, however, is the total opposite: it weighs a great deal even if it is very short in terms of the amount of time that passes. It says in the Hikam, "If someone is given *baraka* in their time, they will be able to obtain in a short period of time more gifts from Allah than can be described through words and gestures."

And when it comes to getting nourishment for their outer forms, they only ever seek what is purest, healthiest and most lawful, for consuming what is lawful illuminates the hearts and gives limbs the strength and energy to obey Allah. And they take it with *lutf*, with kindness and discretion, not jostling for it nor being anxious and greedy nor tiring themselves out on its account. Similarly, when Allah reveals one of the innermost secrets of His Essence to them, they take great care to conceal it so that none of the creatures of Allah know what they have except for those who are worthy. For if they had revealed to them, they would either have stoned them or made them revert to their religion by forcing them to abandon the way of the People, and then they would never know success. All success is from Allah.

Then He mentions the people of the inhabitants of the cave discovering them, saying:

> "Accordingly We made them chance upon them unexpectedly so they might know that Allah's promise is true and that there is no doubt about the Hour. When they were arguing among themselves about the matter, they said, 'Wall up their cave, their Lord knows best about them.' But those who got the better of the argument concerning them said, 'We will build a place of worship over them.' They will say, 'There were three of them, their dog being the fourth.' They will say, 'There were five of them, their dog being the sixth,' guessing at the Unseen. And they will say, 'There were seven of them, their dog being the eighth.' Say: 'My Lord knows best their number. Those who know about them are very few.'" [Al-Kahf: 21-22]

The Haqq says, **"Accordingly"** i.e. In the same way that we put them to sleep and woke them up so that they could grow in certainty, **"We made them chance upon them unexpectedly"** i.e. We made it so that people came upon them and saw them **"so they might know"** i.e. so that the people who were living in the time might know **"that Allah's promise"** i.e. His promise that they will be resurrected and will be either rewarded or punished **"is true"** something that will happen and that nothing can stop from happening, for their sleep and their waking up was very much like one who dies and then is resurrected, **"and that… about the Hour"** i.e. the Rising, which is the way Allah describes the moment that all of mankind is resurrected so that they can be brought to account and receive their recompense, **"…there is no doubt…"** There is no doubt that it will happen. Anyone who saw with their own eyes that Allah took the souls of these young men and held on to them for more than three hundred years, protecting their bodies from decay and decomposition, and then returned them to them just as they were, can no longer be in any doubt whatsoever that Allah's promise is true and that we will be resurrected from our graves and receive recompense for our actions.

This chance discovery happened **"When they were arguing"**, at a time during which they were arguing **"among themselves about the matter,"** about whether the resurrection was going to happen or not. One group of them affirmed it and one group rejected it. Some speculated that only the souls would be resurrected while others said that it would be both body and soul. It is said that the king of the city at the time was a right-acting man who had ruled over them for twenty-eight years. Then the people of his kingdom started to argue with each other about the resurrection in the manner we have described, so the king went into his house and shut the door. Then he put on a coarse woolen frock, sat down upon a pile of ash, and asked his Lord to reveal the truth of the matter to him. So Allah put it in the heart of a man from the land in which the cave was situated to demolish the wall that had been built at the mouth of the cave. So he knocked down the wall that Daqyanus had built to block the entrance to the cave, thinking the cave would be an ideal enclosure in which to keep his flock. And it was at that moment that Allah awoke the people of the cave from their sleep, and they had the conversation among themselves that is described in the *ayas* earlier.

It is narrated that when their man entered the city to buy the food and handed over his silver coins to pay for them, they saw that the coins bore the seal of Daqyanus, so they accused him of having found some buried treasure. So they took him to their king, and he told the king his story. When they heard what he had to say, one of them said, "Our parents told us that some young men fled from Daqyanus on account of their religion. Maybe these are those very men." So the king and his subjects, believers and unbelievers alike, went out from the city to the cave, and went into it and spoke to those inside. Then the young men said to the king, "Farewell! We ask that Allah keep you safe and protect you from men and jinn." And then they returned to their resting places and fell down dead. So the king threw his garment over them, and had a coffin of gold made for each of them. But he saw them later in his sleep and they told him they did not like gold, so he made the coffins out of oak instead. Then he built a place of worship at the mouth of the cave. It is said that when they arrived at the entrance to the cave, the young man said to them, "Wait here and let me go first so they do not become alarmed." So he went inside, and suddenly the entrance became obscured so that they could no longer see it, so they built a place of worship there.

It is also said that the cause of their argument was what had really happened to the young men before they woke up. In other words, 'We made them chance unexpectedly upon them when they were discussing what had happened to the young men and what had transpired between them and Daqyanus, details they had learnt by word of mouth or by the legends told them by their forefathers. Whichever of the two interpretations is correct, the *fa* in Allah's Words *fa-qaalu* - **"they said"** is pure and eloquent. In other words, "We made them chance upon them and they saw what they saw, then the young men died, so some of them said, **"'Wall up their cave"** Build a wall at the entrance of the cave to block them off and prevent people from getting to them. So they did, out of consideration for their rank and to keep them safe and protected.

Then they said, **"their Lord knows best about them.'"** It is as if these words came out of their mouths after they realised that they were unable to learn the truth about them and could not know for sure how many of them there were, what their true lineage was and how long they had remained in the cave. They said these words, handing knowledge of the affair back to the Knower of the Unseen. It is also possible that these are the Words of Allah, said as a response to those who entered into this argument about them without knowledge. **"But those who got the better of the argument concerning them said"** namely, the king and the believers, for they were the ones who got the better of the argument at the time. They said, **"'We will build a place of worship over them.'"** The stories state that, at the entrance to the cave, he built a place of worship in which he used to pray.

Then the discussion moves to the time of our Prophet, may Allah bless him and grant him peace, and the argument between the Christians of Najran and the Muslims. When they came to

Madina, they mentioned the story of the people of the cave and argued with the Muslims regarding how many there were, as Allah reports when He says, **"They will say, 'There were three of them, their dog being the fourth.'"** This is the statement of the Jacobite Christians, and their main representative, as-Sayyid. It is also said to be the position of the Jews. **"They will say, 'There were five of them, their dog being the sixth,'"** This is the statement of the Nestorian Christians, and their main representative, al-'Aqib. **"guessing at the Unseen,"** either making a statement without having learned the reality of the matter, or suspecting something of the Unseen to be so without having ascertained whether it is or not. **"And they will say, 'There were seven of them, their dog being the eighth.'"** This is what the Muslims say, having learned the reality of the affair from this Revelation, for these Words are not laid out in the series of words described as being a guess at the Unseen, and in fact have a different structure to what precedes them, for this statement is preceded by the word *waw* - 'and' and that indicates a greater emphasis on what is said thereafter and that it is the statement that is correct.

Allah says, **"'Say"**, O Muhammad, asserting what is true and refuting the statements of those who spoke first, **"'My Lord knows best their number"** i.e. My Lord's knowledge of their number is greater, **"Those who know about them"** i.e. The people who know how many of them there were **"are very few.'"** Those whom Allah has enabled to reach the truth of the matter through proofs or through inspiration. Ibn Abbas said, "I am one of those few. By Allah inserting the *waw*, He indicates this number is separate from the others, and by Him remaining silent about this number and not qualifying it with the words 'guessing at the Unseen', we know that it is true." And it has been narrated from Ali that there were seven of them and their names were, Yamlikha, the one who went into the city with their silver; Mixelmina, the eldest of them and their spokesman; Mashlina, who in at-Tabari's account is referred to as Majsisiya instead - these three were positioned to the right of the king. As for those on his left, they were Marnush, Dabarnush and Jashadhanus. These six used to advise the king in his affairs. As for the seventh, he was the shepherd who followed them when they fled from Daqyanus, and his name was Kafashtatiyush. On the authority of at-Tabari, Ibn Atiya mentioned a few names different to these, all of which were non-Arab, and then said, "The *isnad* for these names, however, is weak, and Allah knows best."

Ishara: It is Allah's custom with His *awliya* to keep them hidden in the beginning of their affair as a mercy to them, since were He to have made their state known in the beginning of their affair, the common people would have tempted and seduced them and caused them to return from where they started. No, it is only after they have rid themselves of their last remnants and become firmly established in witnessing and direct knowledge of the Haqq, that Allah allows them to be found by those He wants to achieve happiness and arrive to His Presence. By that they will know Allah's promise that there will always be a certain number of *awliya* through whom He keeps the world running, to be true, and that the world will become a ruin when they die out. And they will know that the Hour is coming, not doubt about it. In the *aya*, it lets us know that it is blameworthy to offer opinions about things about which you have no knowledge, and praises those who ascribe knowledge to Allah in every matter. Allah knows best.

Then He commands His Prophet to not engage in argumentation after the truth has been made clear, saying:

"So do not enter into any argument concerning them, except in relation to what is clearly known. And do not seek the opinion of any of them regarding them. Never say about anything, 'I am doing that tomorrow,' without adding 'If Allah wills.' Remember your Lord when you forget, and say, 'Hopefully my Lord will guide me to something closer to right guidance than this.' They stayed in their Cave for three hundred years and added nine. Say: 'Allah knows best how long they stayed. The Unseen of the heavens and the earth belongs to Him. How perfectly He sees, how well He hears! They have no protector apart from Him. Nor does He share His rule with anyone.'" [Al-Kahf: 23-26]

The Haqq says, **"So do not enter into any argument"** i.e. do not enter into a dispute with them **"concerning them"** i.e. the facts surrounding the story of the people of the cave **"except in relation to what is clearly known"** i.e. sticking to the details of the story described and dealt with in the revelation, and not adding anything else, while at all times ascribing knowledge of the affair to Allah. Do not declare them to be ignorant or expose their mistakes, for to do so would be to display a lack of courtesy. **"And do not seek the opinion...regarding them"** i.e. regarding the people of the cave **"...of any of them..."** i.e. of any of those who discuss the matter without knowledge. Because of what has been revealed to you, you have been spared the need. And anyway, they have no knowledge of the matter.

"Never say about anything" i.e with respect to something you have decided to do, **"'I am doing that"** thing **"tomorrow'"** i.e. at some point in the future. *ghaddan* can be used to mean tomorrow or some other time further afield than that. This *aya* was revealed when the Jews said to Quraysh, "Ask him about the *ruh*, the people of the cave and DhulQarnayn." So they asked the Prophet, may Allah bless him and grant him peace, about these things and he replied, "I will tell you about them tomorrow" without qualifying his statement. So the revelation was withheld from him for so long that it became a cause of great distress for him, and Quraysh started to call him a liar. Then, after fourteen days or so had passed, according to the narrations of the people of Sira, this *Sura* was revealed. In other words, do not say, "I am going to do something in some set of circumstances or at some future time, without linking it to His Will in the customary way, and that is by saying, *insha'allah* - 'If Allah wills'." By saying these words, you are acknowledging that it is He who grants you permission to do that action. Your forgetfulness in the matter is also by His Will.

"Remember your Lord" by saying, 'If Allah wills', thereby rectifying your statement **"when you forget"** when it slips your mind and then you remember later. Abdullah ibn Abbas said, "Even if it is after a year, so long as you have not broken your word." It is on this basis that some of the fuqaha have declared it to be permissible to delay the voicing of any exception clause. But the majority of fuqaha disagree, saying that were that to be true, then no divorce or manumission would be binding, and it would be impossible to distinguish truth from falsehood. Al-Qurtubi said, "This is specific to rectifying an omission and righting a wrong. As for qualifications that change the ruling completely, they must be said in the moment and cannot be delayed." It is also possible that the meaning is, "Remember your Lord by glorifying Him and asking His forgiveness whenever you forget to qualify your statements with the words 'If Allah wills'", thereby emphatically emphasising their importance. Another possible meaning is, "Remember your Lord when forgetfulness strikes, to make right whatever has passed." It has also been interpreted to refer to the ruling that you must make up missed prayers as soon as you remember them. These words will be discussed further in the *ishara* that follows.

"and say, 'Hopefully my Lord will guide me to" will grant me the success to receive **"something closer…than this."** i.e. an account that is closer and more readily apparent than the account of the people of the cave, and serves even better as a sign and proof of my Prophethood, **"…to right guidance…"** i.e. right guidance for the people. And Allah did as he requested, revealing *ayas* to him that were even greater and brought even more clarity to the stories of Prophets who lived in the distant past, and *ayas* that told him of things that were in the Unseen and had not yet come to pass, details of future epochs right up until the coming of the Hour.

Or the *aya* means something better and closer to right guidance than the thing that was forgotten. In other words, "Hopefully my Lord will guide me to something that has more benefit in it for me than that which I forgot," since it is possible that a person forgetting can be the source of more good for him than his remembering, since that demonstrates Allah's overwhelming power, His having no need for His creation, and His unconcern as to whether people come running to Him or turn away.

Or by "something closer to right guidance than this", Allah is referring to a path that is closer to right guidance than that followed by the people of the cave, and Allah did indeed do that, for He guided the Prophet, may Allah bless him and grant him peace, to the straight Deen that He exalted over every other deen, though the *mushrikun* hate it.

"**They stayed in their Cave**" alive, with their ears sealed with sleep, "**for three hundred years and added nine.**" It has been narrated that Ali ibn Abi Talib said, "According to the people of the Book, they remained there for three hundred solar years. But Allah refers to lunar years, and the difference between the two is three years for every hundred years, so that makes it three hundred and nine lunar years." "**Say: 'Allah knows best how long they stayed.'**" i.e. the length of time they spent in the cave. "**The Unseen of the heavens and the earth belongs to Him**" i.e. the things that are kept concealed from the inhabitants of the heavens and the earth and which they cannot see. "**How perfectly He sees, how well He hears!**" By using an interjection denoting wonder, Allah indicates that His hearing and His sight are totally unlike our own, for nothing can obscure His sight. For Him, there are no barriers, there is no difference between thick and thin, large and small, hidden and manifest. Wonder when used in reference to Allah is merely metaphorical, since it is something that manifests itself only when someone is confronted by something whose cause is unknown, and since awe and astonishment are only felt by someone who sees something which he is not used to, and Allah is exalted above that. So it is interpreted as an emphatic way of saying that His sight and His hearing encompass absolutely everything, as we said earlier.

"**They have no protector apart from Him**" i.e. the inhabitants of the heavens and the earth have no protector other than Him, have no one to support them or take care of their affairs except for Him. "**Nor does He share His rule**" His determining of and knowledge of matters in the Unseen, "**with anyone**" with any of them, and does not grant any of them a way. One of the readings has this in the second person - in other words, 'O you who hears these Words, do not think that any of His creation share with Him in His rule and management of affairs. Allah knows best.

Ishara: Five of the qualities of the *Sufiyya* are indicated within these *ayas*:

1. The avoidance of argumentation and dispute, except when it is in the form of discussion and debate in order to bring out the truth. This should not be done with quarrelling and the raising of voices, but instead with gentleness, kind words and in good spirits.

2. Seeking a fatwa of the heart whenever any matter arises. The Prophet said, "Seek a fatwa of your heart even if the muftis have already given you their fatwas, for good is that in which the heart finds peace and tranquility, while iniquity is that which gives the heart pause and causes it unease." The hearts that are referred to here, the hearts that are consulted, are those hearts which have been purified and illuminated by the remembrance of Allah, and have renounced and forsaken all that is other than Him. Such hearts only feel clear and at ease in the presence of truth, unlike hearts that are caught up in love of this world and its whim and caprices - the only fatwas they give are ones which accord with their whims and appetites.

3. Submitting to the Will of Allah, handing the management of your affairs over to Him and being content with whatever your Decree has in store for you. In other words, you do

not make any plan or decide upon doing anything without acknowledging that is by the Will of Allah - you look to see what Allah will do with you. When the person of intellect wakes up, he looks to what Allah will do with him, while the one who is ignorant looks to what he can do with himself, as the author of the Hikam said.

4. Occupying your time with *dhikr* and reflection until you withdraw from all that is other than the Remembered. Allah says, "**Remember your Lord when you forget**" i.e. When you have forgotten all that is other than Him, you have truly become one who remembers. True remembrance is that which takes you away from yourself, from seeing your form and your senses, to such a degree that when you speak, it is the Haqq speaking, so complete is your withdrawal. This is witnessed firsthand by those who find a Shaykh of Instruction and keep close company with him.

5. Seeking to advance and increase in right guidance and certainty. Every time you reach a station, you look to reach a station higher than it, for there is no end to His knowledge nor His greatness ("**And say, 'Hopefully my Lord will guide me to something closer to right guidance than this.'**"). All success lies with Allah.